MOMMA, PLEASE FORGIVE ME!

by
Toi L. Moore

TM Publications
Colton, California, USA

Momma, Please Forgive Me!
by: Toi Moore

All Rights Reserved.   Copyright 2001, Toi Moore

COVER ARTIST:
Brian Olsen
B O ILLuStRaToR@aol.com

COVER DESIGN:
D'Graphics Publications, Inc.
dgraphics1@juno.com

ISBN 0-9713221-0-4
First Printing, October 2001
10 9 8 7 6 5 4 3 2 1

Copyright Toi Moore, 2001
Printed in the United States of America

Published by:
TM PUBLICATIONS
P.O. Box 443
Colton, CA 92324
http://www.ToiMoore.com
TMPublications1@aol.com

PUBLISHER'S NOTE:

This is a work of fiction. Names, characters, places, and incidents either are the products of the author's imagination or are used fictitiously, and any resemblance to actual persons, living or dead, events, or locales is entirely coincidental.

All rights reserved. No part of this book may be reproduced, stored in or introduced into a retrieval system, or transmitted, in any form, or by any means (electonic, mechanical, photocopying, recording, or otherwise), without written permission of both the copyright owner and the publisher, except in the case of quotes used in critical articles and reviews.

DEDICATION

I would like to dedicate this book to my loving and wonderful husband
Gregory David Moore
You have always stood by my side when no one else cared. You laughed with me and you held me in your arms when I cried. You've been my best friend, husband, lover and the best father a man can be to our two sons. You've always encouraged me to reach for my goals and work toward my dreams while never giving up. You've encouraged me to be strong when the going was tough. You've taught me how to turn my ears away from the naysayer's, who didn't think I could fulfill my dreams or reach my goals. You've always loved me no matter what! For that, I will always love you dearly and I will always be grateful for your love, support and constant encouragement! God knew what he was doing when he sent you to me. You were truly sent from heaven above! I Love You Forever!

Toi

SPECIAL THANK YOU'S TO MY CHARTER MEMBERS

I would like to gave a special thanks to those of you who believed in me when I only had a dream. All of you put your money where your mouth was when it was needed the most. Due to your love, kindness, encouragement and contributions, I was able to fulfill my dream by self-publishing this book. I want all of you to know that I will always hold a special place in my heart for each of you, knowing that you were there in the beginning of a journey that will exceed distances I never imaged. I wish each and everyone of you peace, love, happiness and the joy of also fulfilling your greatest dreams and desires. My prayers will always be with you. Don't let anyone tell you that you can't! Let the word **can't** be totally eliminated from your vocabulary. Always know that the sky is our only limit and God can give us the world if we work hard and aim toward our dreams and goals!

Gregory Moore, Kenan Moore, Amon Moore, Harriette and George Parker, Wilma Westmoreland, Muriel Darling, Evonte Moore, Michele McDowell, Michael Minor, Eric Anderson, Stanley and Ivy Westmoreland, Rhonda Shaw-Beard, Candy King, Donovan and Diane Carter, Tefere and Jan Hazey, Evelia Sands, Bruce Gordon, Sheila Glenn, Lillie Anderson, Rita Jackson, James and Charles Etta Jackson, Frances Wilson, Alan and Lekili Hubbard, Sheryl and Land Richards, Lori Parker, Jamille Goodall, Robert and Cynthia Hooks, Edward and Noreena Ramos, Brenton Woods, Monica Jackson, Florence and William Parrott, Betty and James Daniels, Jane Luper, Patricia Blake, Sonya Parker, Criss Draper, Jeannie Washington, Christine Bias, Charles McVay & Erlinda Garcia

In loving memory of those very precious to me and have gone on in search of the light, I miss you!

'Grandma,' Idora Cook, 'Nana,' Willie Mae Watson, 'Daddy,' James R. Blake, 'Nanny' & 'Granddaddy,' Gladys & Sam Blake, 'Cousin,' Stanley Westmoreland II

ACKNOWLEDGMENTS

I would like to first and foremost thank my heavenly father, *God!* Without you, nothing is possible! Thank you God for your constant love and support. Thank you for giving me a mind to think clearly and the gift of being able to express myself in words. Thank you for helping me find my gift of writing and allowing me to spread your word. I have always known and recognized where my blessings come from and will continue giving you the glory, honor and praise. Thank you God! I would like to thank my two very handsome son's, *Kenan* and *Amon*, for your love and support. I would also like to thank you guys for turning down the television and music when I needed the house to be quiet. I would like to thank my mother, *Wilma Westmoreland* for always loving me and helping me learn many valuable lessons as a child that I feel have made me a better adult, for those foundations I am most proud. I love you! My sister *Niko Hankerson* I love you, and always remember that the entire universe is yours for the taking, just grab it and hold on. My brother *Eric Anderson*, with all the odds against you as a child, I thank God that you rose above and became a survivor, strong and successful, I love you! It's amazing to know that the hand is quicker than the eye while watching you do magic. My mother-in law, *Muriel Darling*, thank you for always supporting me and encouraging me to continue with my dream, while always pushing me to go forth. Thank you for seeing my dream from day one and buying my first word processor so that I could write my first story that lead to many others. *Evonte Moore*, thank you for being a great brother-in-law and always supporting and encouraging my dream. *Harriette Parker*, my other sister, thank you for always encouraging, supporting and believing in me enough to inspire others to put their money where their mouth was! *George Parker*, I'll never forget that dance at my birthday party, thank you for being you and always being there to support me! *Michele McDowell*, my long time friend and sister, thanks for the GREAT ideas in helping me put this story together, along with the valuable background ideas needed to help make this story real and exciting. Also, thanks for taking the time to read my work when I needed another eye. *Michael Minor*, thanks for offering your support when I asked for your opinion on how to get my goal accomplished. *Florence Parrott*, thanks for being a true friend. Your love and support throughout the many years has been great and will never be forgotten. You've always been there for me and I thank you for that! *Bill* and *Danny*, thanks for all the computer help you gave me when I couldn't figure what the heck was going on. *Brian Olsen* thanks so very much for designing such a creative and touching book cover. I know I gave you a hard time, but you hung in there to the end. Now, aren't you proud of your hard work and my push!:) *Lori Olsen,* thanks for working on the day I made copies, "Looking for Artist." Your brother was a life saver! I'm glad you hooked us up! *Rhonda Shaw-Beard* and *Dr. Letitia Wright* thank you so very much for your in-dept editing and great suggestions of my work. *Letitia*, thanks for your friendship and letting me get coverage on your television show. *Terry Boykins*, thanks for the great marketing ideas. With my talents and your marketing strategies, I'm bound to be a millionaire! *Patricia Blake*, thanks for being a great aunt and always offering words of encouragement. *Dr. Keith O. Hilton* and the *Precinct Reporter Newspaper,* thank you for giving me my first opportunity of becoming published. If it weren't for you, I may have stopped writing and believing in my talents, so thanks for encouraging me to continue. *Bishop Dr. George Mc Kinney,* thanks for the wonderful words and lessons learned about God and allowing me to have a firm foundation in his word. *Sister Mc Kinney,* I send my love! *Maureen Heuring-Appel,* thanks for allowing me the opportunity of doing what I do best, write and get paid! While writing for **The Cause** and **Saludos Hispanos Magazines** over the years has been great! I'll always treasure with great pride and appreciation the many adventures and exposure you've allowed me to share with the world. *Gail Mitchell*, thank you for allowing my writing to be viewed by a whole new world and gaining a new respect in what I do while writing for Billboard Magazine. I'm hanging with the big boys now!:) *Maria Alamillo,* thanks for introducing me to *Gail* and giving me some great interviews. It does help to know the right people. *Jacquelin Thomas*, thank you for showing me how to structure my book properly when others told me to figure it out on my own. *Uncle Stan* and *Ivy*, thanks for always being there, no matter what! Thanks for the continued love and support throughout my entire life, while always encouraging me and never putting me down. *James* and *Debbie Ingram, Vivica A. Fox, Patrice Rushen* and *T. C. Carson*, thanks for your love and continued support. Thanks for allowing me the opportunity of sharing your words of encouragement in my writing to the world. *Patrice Rushen*, thanks for all of your love, support, friendship and encouragement over the many years. Also, thanks for the many interviews you gave me whenever I called. *Debbie Ingram*, over the many years you've always encouraged me to strive toward my goal and never give up. You've always expressed how proud you were of me as I reached toward each step of my goal. I will always be grateful for your love. *James Ingram*, thanks for always giving my husband work! *Vivica A. Fox* and *T.C. Carson*, thanks for coming through for me whenever I called, it means a lot! *Partice Reed*, thanks for your constant help and encouragement. Also, thanks for sharing in the excitement when I had good news to share, it encouraged both of us to work harder toward reaching our goals. You are someone I know will always be there for me, thanks. *Treva Jackson*, thanks for your longgggg time friendship. Girl, since elementary school you have been my friend, encouraging me all the way, thanks! *Sister Shah'Keyah*, thanks for all of your help, which has truly been a blessing. You came through for me out of the goodness of your heart and I will always appreciate and admire your giving nature. I have adopted you as my new sister-friend. Thanks *Charles Love* for introducing us, even when you thought we were going to plot against you guys while you were away in Italy. Us women do have to stick together!:) I can't wait for the wedding, hurry up! *Candi King, Phyllis Robinson, Celeste E. Willams, Cathy Kidd, Evelia Sands*, and *Venus McDowell*, thanks for reading and/or editing my work, past or present, and sharing your thoughts. *Juanita Thomas*, thanks for your friendship. *Lois, Lorraine, Kim, Darcy, Marlo, Nolan, Janice, Darnell, nieces and nephews*, thanks for your love. *Dr. Betty Daniels, M.D.*, thanks for getting rid of those CRAZY cramps! You're the best GYN any girl could ask for! *Cherise, Lori, Reggie* and all the staff members at the San Bernardino *Office Depot*, thanks for making my many office visits fun and personal. *Faron and Joann Roberts* at Phenix Information Center, thanks for your words of advice and knowledge whenever I asked. *Charles McVay,* thanks for approving my car loan when my credit wouldn't allow that large amount.:) *Vanessa Brown*, thanks for putting the word out on what I'm doing in your IE Calendar. To all of you who have loved and encouraged me throughout my life, know that I thank and love you back with all my heart and soul!

Toi

ABOUT THE AUTHOR

Toi was born and raised in San Diego, California. If you hear the sound of her voice, you'd swear she was from the south. Nevertheless, she's just a plain ole' city girl. She has been a wife for over 17 years, and is the mother of two young boys. Her interest in writing started at a very young age. She would write notes of inspiration to friends and family members on birthday's or holidays. During that time, Toi did not take her writing seriously, nor had she recognized her gift, which was given from God.

While a senior in high school, she wrote a poem titled "I Remember." After writing this poem, she put it away, too afraid to show anyone. Ten years later, that very poem became published in the high school memory book, in honor of her ten year class reunion. This was the first time her work had been published. After seeing her work in print, she was encouraged to pursue writing more seriously, which lead to her writing more poems and stories.

Her genuine interest in writing immediately occurred after hearing the words of famed romance writer Judith Kranz. On a popular television talk show, Ms. Kranz spoke words of encouragement and how anyone could write if they just put their mind to what they are doing. At that very moment, Toi decided to farther her skills in writing by creating a short story. This story was a steamy romance titled "No Words Were Spoken." After its completion, Toi shared it with several family and friends. Their overwhelming and positive responses assured her that she was on the right track. In fact, their response confirmed she was on the track, inspired by God. However, after reading Terry McMillan's book, 'Waiting to Exhale,' she was farther encouraged to write with an added ethic cultural and sassy flair.

After this confirmation, she went on to write

several short stories, along with becoming a staff writer for many newspaper and magazine publications. Currently, she is writing for Billboard Magazine. Her talents also lead to her interest in writing her first novel, with others that have followed. Since her awakening of her gift to write, her talents have allowed her credits to include over 200 published articles in various newspaper and magazines throughout the United States and Canada. She also adds to her credit several short stories and four novels. Toi has also worn the hat of publisher, as she published her own magazine titled "Mini Romances." This magazine was designed to allow a voice for new and unpublished writers.

Toi has several bylines to her credit in which she has authored and/or interviewed a variety of well-known celebrities such as: Oprah Winfrey, James Ingram, Vivica A. Fox, Jermaine Dupri, Leila Ali, Synthia St. James, "Sugar" Shane Mosely, Boney James, Regina Belle, Malcolm-Jamal Waner, Marilyn McCoo & Billy Davis, Jr., Jaheim, Danny Glover, Patti LaBelle, Patrice Rushen, Lamont Dozier, Howard Hewett, Eric Jerome Dickey, Michael DeLorenzo, NAACP Chairman Kweisi Mfume, Maya Angelou, and Tupac Shakur to name a few. While composing these stories, she has covered a wide range of subjects such as: entertainment, health, religion, politics, sports, education, and children's issues. Her experience, faith and hard work make her an experienced and well-rounded writer.

Today, she continues her writings, while realizing and accepting her gift from God. She realizes that discovering your gift is precious within itself, therefore, grab onto it and hold tight until you've made your way to the top. The love and support from her family and friends is what continues to motivate her in her continued journey, while never accepting no for an answer.

PREFACE

This story deals with domestic violence and how it can be a silent killer. It's a silent killer, because those who are silent are often the ones who get killed! The killing either takes place, and is shown on their physical body with scars or death, or it affects and destroys their mind.

Oftentimes, a persons spirit becomes the innocent victim of this deadly problem. It affects many people in different ways, often with outsiders never knowing any details, or its severity in the lives it affects.

This story also deals with how domestic violence is intensified with the use of drugs and alcohol, often leaving chilling results.

The original story idea for this book was conceived during the fall of 1993. It started as a ten page short story I wrote to submit in a contest. When I refect back to the day I wrote those first ten pages, I remember crying. The words were so strong and the story was so real. I did not know anyone who resembled the character I wrote, nor did I know anyone personally who had been through her pain, all I did know was that it was real. The voice of Mariah Carey's song, *"Hero,"* was being played over and over in the background that night. Those words were so powerful and so true; *"That a hero comes along, looking for you to be strong. Then you finally see the truth, that the hero lies in you!"* Those very words sung, along with the message within my story made me know for sure that no matter what situation a person is faced with, large or small, that hero lies only within you!

After writing my touching story, I went on to write

others. However, the power of its content stayed deep within my soul for several years. Due to the serious nature of the story and the powerful vibes I felt from its content, I knew I had to expand it much more.

I grew up in a family that had a continuing cycle of domestic violence. The occurred violence in my immediate family had nothing to do with drugs or alcohol, only great pain and violence. At the time, I was only 6 years old. I was a child who hid behind the doors and walls of our home while my mother endured great pain. I did not know what to do, who to call, or how to help. I was afraid for myself and my mother, fearing I would be next.

After becoming an adult, I realized that I had blocked out the length of the abuse, leaving only a faint memory of the cries and screams I heard while being a helpless victim. I too became the victim, because my mother's pain hurt me dearly. I feel that these violent acts only occurred because power and control was needed in the relationship.

I also received several disciplined beatings from my step-father's powerful hands. One of his beatings left me with thick-green bruises on my legs. They were so deep that I had to wear long pants or stockings to school for an entire week in order to cover up the scars and pain endured to my petite and fragile body! Shortly after, my mother gained enormous strength and courage to stand up to her abuser and stop the abuse. She drew the line when it came to hurting me and stood her ground by putting him out, saying; "No More!" Life became happy, knowing he was gone for good!

Due to the pain and suffering during those dark days, I can still hear, see and feel the pain my mother endured at the hands of her abuser. Those days we'll never forget!

Due to that experience, the children in my story were very real as I wrote this book. Due to those dark memories, I swore that I would never endure the kind of pain my mom once felt from the hands of an abuser, by breaking the cycle. Thanks to God and a conscience decision made by me and my husband, the vicious cycle has stopped, sparing myself and my children from that kind of hurt and pain, as I refuse to endure or accept abuse, or allow it to grow in my household.

During the year of 2000, the story was still buried deep inside my soul. So, I uncovered the desire and wrote my first screenplay, which defined more details that stemmed from my original ten page story. After completing the screenplay, I still felt that the story didn't quite draw the completed picture of how domestic violence not only affects the adults who endure the pain, but the children who witness its severity as well, so I wrote this book.

After writing this detailed story, I now feel that many can understand and agree that domestic violence is nothing to overlook, because it affects many who bear the scars forever.

We must all try to prevent any and all acts of domestic violence, mental or physical, by not allowing it to be acceptable in our lives. If we don't take a stand, the stand will take place in our lives and in the lives of our children forever, allowing the cycle to continue! We must put a stop to this deadly and hurtful disease once and for all! No one has a good reason to become an abuser, or to be abused! No one has to put their hands on someone to prove a point! Think about it, then do something about it to stop it!

Toi

MOMMA, PLEASE FORGIVE ME!

by
Toi L. Moore

Momma, Please Forgive Me!

CHAPTER ONE

"I hate you! I hate you! Take your hands off of me and get away right now! I'm not going to let you do this to me again. No more, never again!" La Vonne Brown said in fear as Jonathan, her drug induced husband beat her while her small children watched with fear.

"I told you not to call the cops, but you wouldn't listen. La Vonne, all I wanted you to do was love me as your husband. But all you ever did was complain and nag me about the things I wasn't doing. The only thing I did was have a good time with my friends. But now that you've called the cops, you're gonna pay!" Then he continued to beat her, socking her in the face with his fist and in her stomach while she cried with great agony.

"Stop Daddy! Don't hit mommy! Please stop now before you hurt her like you did before." Jonathan Jr. said as his dad continued hitting his mother who only weighted 105 pounds, next to his dad's giant 210 pound body. The powerful blows from his fist caused her face to bleed.

"Get away from me you little bastard." Jonathan Sr. said as he pushed away his eight year old son. "You better take your black ass back to bed before I put my foot up in it!" Then he looked at La Vonne, who was a small-framed light skinned black woman. She was trying to wipe away the blood that dripped from her face while holding her stomach that was cramping from the pain. The cramping was a result of not only the pain she endured from the beating, but from the fragileness her body was in while carrying their unborn twins in her womb. While bearing the massive pain, La Vonne noticed trickles of blood running down her leg. To her surprise, it was leaking from her vagina, where her babies were sheltered away from the world.

Jonathan looked at the blood and became more enraged with what he saw and screamed; "We didn't need no more damn kids around here anyway! I hope the little bastard's die!" Then he let out a sound of laughter that was pulled up from the bottom of his stomach, shook his head and continued to smile. He was feeling proud of what he had done. His large frame towered over La Vonne and her children. His size and dark complexion skin color gave him a power and strength that frighten many who were in his presence.

After hearing her fathers harst words, Stacy, their six year old daughter ran back to her bedroom while crying out loud. Jr. sat in silence. "Jonathan just leave him alone, you're scaring him." La Vonne warned, as he prepared to teach their son a lesson. "Don't you dare put your hands on him." Fear and rage was deeply embedded in her voice. "Just leave us alone. Go back with your friends! Just leave this house!"

As she stood in pain holding her stomach, her thoughts focused on the police actually coming to her rescue, even though she knew that wasn't likely to happen. She knew that this time was different and that this time things were very wrong. However, the reality was always the same, the police only came in her neck of the woods if someone was bleeding to death or worse. By living in a low class neighborhood that was predominately African-American, resulted in the less than fair treatment and respect given by anyone with authority.

As La Vonne stood there, Jr. saw the fear in his mothers eyes. He wanted to help. "Daddy just leave us alone! We didn't do anything to you." He fearfully said. Suddenly, Jonathan held up his hand and hit his son right in the face, making his lip bleed. Jr. fell to the beat-up wooden floor and began crying. He held his nose, trying to stop the blood from streaming down.

Jonathan laughed out loud as he watched his son laying on the floor. "Get off that floor you little sissy. What's the matter, you

Momma, Please Forgive Me!

can't take it like a man? Your ass been hanging around your damn momma for too long. She got you acting like a little bitch. That's all you are is a little bitch-ass momma's boy. Get your ass off that damn floor and stop crying like a little baby."

Jr. stayed on the floor, ignoring his father's threats. He feared that if he stood up, his father would knock him down again. "Did you hear me you little bastard? I said get the fuck up right now before I hit you again!" Jr. tried to slowly stand up, but the pain was too bad, causing him to drop back down to the floor. Jonathan shook his head and laughed as he watched his son struggle.

Suddenly La Vonne's pain faded away. After seeing the look on her son's face, listening to the words that came from her husband's mouth and the laughter that came from his body, her facial expressions turned from fear to rage. She dropped down to her living room floor and held her grieving son tight in her arms. She rocked him back and forth, close to her body, trying to ease away the pain. "Shhh, don't cry. It's alright, it'll be alright." As she held him tight, the blood on her face continued to drip down from the painful blow to her nose she endured from the beating Jonathan had forced upon her, mixing both of their bloods together.

"Now, are you satisfied? Are you satisfied that you can beat us all up? You're such a big man now. Jonathan just leave! Leave us alone and get out of our house. We don't want you here anymore. I'm tired of going though all this pain. I'm tired of my kids watching you beat on me every night. I'm also tired of the broken bones and the black eyes you've given me through the years. I've had enough! So do us all a favor and leave." she warned agin. After recognizing the violent acts of what her kids were constantly witnessing, La Vonne suddenly began to feel strong and unafraid. Due to this constant hurt and pain they witnessed, she knew the violence had to come to an end.

"Bitch, don't talk to me like that!" Jonathan said with a devilish fire in his eyes. "Who do you think you are? Ain't no motha'-fucker going to tell me what to do in my own house, and I mean no damn body!" Slowly, he wobbled his drug induced body to the couch, sat down, closed his eyes and fell fast asleep. As he slept, he proudly wore a sarcastic smile on his face.

As La Vonne watched him sleep, displaying his smile of pride, she became filled with rage like never before. While she looked into the eyes of her bleeding son, her rage continued to grow stronger. Due to the dead silence that was now in the house, Stacy gathered up her nerve and peaked around the corner. She wanted to make sure that everybody was alright. After spotting what appeared to be calm, she walked into the living room and sat close to her mother and brother, holding on tight to her mother's arm while sucking her thumb and keeping her eyes focused dead on her sleeping father.

Stacy also attempted to help comfort her brother. She rubbed her hand across his arm and patted him to calm down. After knowing that Jr. was content, La Vonne found a nearby pillow and placed it under his head. Then she slowly struggled through her pain to get off the floor. After raising her limp body up to her knees, she clenched her teeth together and held on to the bottom of her stomach that bared extreme pain. The blood that had slowly dripped from her vagina was the beginning stages of her body hemorrhaging from the six month old twins she was carrying inside of her womb.

However, her feelings of pain were put on hold because she knew that this abuse had to somehow end. Since standing was too painful, she crawled her weakened body toward the couch where Jonathan laid asleep. Then she carefully and quietly reached under the couch, searching for her answer. As she stretched her arm farther and farther, she felt the presence of what she knew was her savior. This was the answer she believed would solve all of her problems.

Finally, La Vonne's desperate search was over as she pulled out a long gauged shot gun. Her small and weak body almost made it impossible for her to hold the heavy gun. After retrieving the weapon, she slowly stood straight to her feet, leaned against a nearby chair for support, placed the gun in position, put her eye on the target, pulled back the trigger and aimed the gun directly toward Jonathan's chest.

After gathering the needed strength and courage, she pulled the trigger back as far as she could, accumulating all the strength that was left in her weakened body and let it go, "Pow!" One shot was all that was heard as the power of the gun made La Vonne fall to the ground, releasing the gun from her hands. It left the loud sound of the heavy metal rifle hitting the hard-wood floor and the smell and smoke of gunpowder floating in the air. After regaining enough strength to look at what she had done, Jonathan's injured body had fallen to the floor, while blood rapidly splattered out from the his chest. She realized that her shot had instantly killed her husband in cold blood as their children watched in fear and disbelief.

At that moment, La Vonne felt no pain. Fear was the farthest thing from her mind. The only thing that was going on in her mind was that he was gone and that he would never be able to harm her or her children again. Her actions brought a sense of relief and calm to her presence. By shooting the man she once loved, and the father of her children, justified her years of pain and abuse that they had suffered in vain.

Suddenly, the reality of what she had just done set firmly in her mind; "Oh my God, what have I done? Lord God, what have I done?" La Vonne hysterically yelled over and over. "What have I done?"

As Jonathan laid on the floor, covered in a pool of blood Stacy and Jr. began crying and screaming; "Mommy, Mommy! What happened to daddy? Mommy, is daddy alright?" they said with curiosity and confusion as their innocent minds protected them from the truth.

The tension in the room was at its height. La Vonne paced back and forth. She was trying to understand what she had done. Her mind suddenly rewound back to her previously attempted phone calls to the police. However, she didn't worry. She knew from past experiences they wouldn't come. While contemplating her thoughts and listening to the cries of her children, she panicked and ran out the house. Her weakened body would not allow her to run fast, but her mental attempts were those of a track star. As she ran, she was yelling and screaming as loud as her voice would travel. "What have I done? Lord, what have I done?" Her screams alerted neighbors, causing them to become fearful and concerned.

As she ran down the street screaming, neighbors came out of their houses. A few of them were already outside, as they had heard the loud sound of the shotgun blast. While La Vonne ran, through her tears, she noticed the blurred vision of flashing red lights in the distance, this time the police were responding. Sirens were roaring and the flashing red lights were beginning to come from every direction. The surrounding neighbors had called for help after hearing the loud gunshot blast and screams.

"La Vonne, don't run, you're the victim," a neighbor yelled out. "Come back, it'll be alright. La Vonne, come back."

After noticing her frantic movements while running away from the area, a police car raced toward her direction. Then it stopped directly in her path. From the reports he was following, La Vonne matched the exact description of his search. He had reached a conclusion that she was the one who had just left the scene of the crime. "Stop Miss, stop right there Miss." Were the words

Momma, Please Forgive Me!

that came from the voice behind the loud speaker of the police car. "Stop right there Miss or I'll shoot." He pulled out his gun and aimed it in her direction.

After realizing what was happening, and acknowledging the pain that was crying out to her weakened and fragile body, La Vonne slowed down and stopped running, falling down to the street. Unsure of her actions, the police slowly approached her, still with his gun aimed directly at her. "You have the right to remain silent." Were the forceful words coming from his mouth as he reached down to handcuff her. "Anything you say or do can and will be held against you."he continued.

As the officer read La Vonne her rights, he raised her limp body up straight where she stood in disbelief as blood continued to slowly run down her legs. She was still hemorrhaging from her pregnancy. Her actions were those of someone who was lifeless or unaware of what had happened. She appeared to be totally unaware of her actions and the blood. The thoughts in her mind were not located on earth, but somewhere lost in space.

As the police placed her in his car, she heard the faint cries of her children calling out her name; "Mommy! Mommy come back! Mommy, please come back. Come back and see about daddy. He's hurt really bad!" they said with an innocent tone.

As La Vonne heard their soft little voices, reality set in as to what she had just done. "Oh my God! Why did I have to kill him. All I wanted to do was stop him from hurting us again. Lord, why did I do it? I didn't mean to kill him."

Then the police pushed her head into the car, slammed the door shut and drove away. As the car drove away, La Vonne turned toward the rear window and watched her children fade into the night. They were standing at their front door aggressively crying for their mom to come back home. Yet the sounds of their cries were silent to her ears as the police car drove farther away.

The only sounds heard were those that were her own. "Let me out of here! My babies need me. Let me out of here!" She yelled.

"Shut up all that damn noise." One cell mate yelled. "Yeah, shut up, I'm trying to sleep." Another cell mate yelled, awakening La Vonne from her nightmare.

Sweating, shaking and out of breath from her nightmare, La Vonne was locked away in the Louisiana State Prison. She was unaware and disillusioned as to where she laid resting. La Vonne was reliving the dreadful night that sent her away to prison, leaving her without her family.

This was a routine she often relived, beginning the first day she arrived. "Oh my God I miss my babies so much," she said as she tried to rock herself back to sleep. "It's been over two years since I've seen or heard their little voices. I wish I could see them again. I know they're alright, because they're with Momma. My only other prayer now is that one day soon Momma will forgive me and bring my babies here to see me." Then La Vonne rolled over and attempted to go back to sleep.

CHAPTER TWO

The night is cold. La Vonne's mother, Gloria, is sitting by her fireplace rocking in her favorite chair. She has just finished reading her bible and begins praying; "Oh Lord God, please give me the strength I need to get by. Give me the heart to one day forgive La Vonne of her sins." Then she looked up to God and laid her bible down on the coffee table by her side.

As she laid her bible down, she noticed a letter on the table. This was the one letter she had saved from her daughter, after returning all the others. For some reason Gloria felt that she was finally able to read the words from La Vonne. For some reason

Momma, Please Forgive Me!

she felt that it was time.

"Hi Momma, it's me La Vonne. After 28 years of my life, remembering your normal nightly routine, I can imagine that you're sitting in your big wooden rocking chair, in front of a burning fireplace. I know that you're looking up to God, praying for your family, especially for the ones who are not safe at home with you, like me."

"I can also imagine that during this same daily prayer, tonight is different. After two long years of rejecting my letters, I've prayed that someday you'd open just one. So, if this letter is not returned to me, I thank you now for finally gathering enough strength and courage to hear my cries while I plead for your forgiveness.

"This is the same letter that I've sent to you for the last two years. The only difference is that I've added a few more words each time it's returned. Then I reseal it in a new envelope, hoping for the best. Momma, I vowed to continue sending my explanation to you until the day you gain enough strength and courage to open just one letter. My words are those that I've prayed you'd understand. Hopefully by now you're ready to accept, or at least understand my reality of taking the life of another human being. Momma, I know that doing such a thing is something you could've never imagined, as you taught me to love all of God's children.

"I know that right now you're looking at your Bible, which is laying by your side. You've always relied on its strength to give you what you need in order to go on. Your strength and faith in God has always held the key that has allowed us to maintain our strength. But on that dreadful day, my strength failed. Momma, please forgive me for the terrible mistake I made. Please bare with me, while I try to explain why I did what I did."

Suddenly ten year old Jr. came running out of his bedroom, rubbing his sleepy eyes. "Grandma, can I have a drink of water?"

he said as he walked into the living room.

"Sure you can sweety. You can have anything you want. Grandma will see to it." Gloria said with reassuring and comforting words as she went to the kitchen and gave her grandson a drink of water in his favorite *Pokemon* cup.

"Thank you Grandma." He said with a smile on his face as he drank his water.

Then, they went back into the living room and Gloria sat down in her chair. After she sat down, Jr. climbed into her lap and gave her a big hug. "Grandma, I was so scared when the police took Mommy away. Thank you for not leaving us alone, and letting us live with you while mommy and daddy are gone."

Then Gloria gave him a big hug while holding back tears. "Baby, Grandma will always be here for you and your sister. Grandma will also make sure that you're safe and no one harms either of you."

"Grandma, do you think it'll be ok if I tell the kids you're my mother instead of my Grandma, since our mom is not here and we don't have a daddy anymore? You can be my momma until my real mom comes home. That way, when the kids talk about their mother's, I can say that my mom is at home. Then they won't tease me or call my mom a killer." Jr. said with a serious look.

Gloria was surprised by his comment; "Sure baby. If that'll make you feel better, you can tell them that I'm your mom."

He looked at Gloria and smiled, kissing her on the cheek. Then he jumped off her lap and started walking toward his room to go back to bed. "Goodnight mom, I love you."

With a big smile, Gloria responded; "I love you too. Goodnight." Then she went back to reading her letter.

"Momma, I want to tell you that I'm sorry for letting you down. What I did was something totally against your beliefs and guidance. If I could only have your forgiveness, everything else would be alright. Momma, I just couldn't handle my situation anymore. I couldn't handle the fussing and fighting. I especially couldn't handle the drugs and alcohol that Jonathan brought into our home. It was because of those drugs that our family became shattered, with no way to fix the damage. It was because of my precious little babies that I had to put a stop to his destruction."

"Momma, I would come home from work and discover that he had sold our personal things just to support his habit. So tell me, how was I supposed to explain that to my kids about all the missing things he took, especially when he stole valuable toys from them? How were they supposed to understand what he did when I couldn't understand myself? Toward the end, I warned him that if he ever walked into our house and beat me or stole from us again, he wouldn't live to see another day.

"Momma, you know that I was always a person that stood up to her words, especially when my kids were the ones suffering the most. Well, on that dreadful night, while Jr. and Stacy watched him beat me again, I did exactly what I said I would do, I blew him away! Unfortunately, that wasn't the right thing to do. But at the time that was the only thing I knew would stop him and save our lives.

"Momma, the night that I shot him was different than all the rest. That night he'd mixed alcohol and drugs together. His actions made me think about Rosalee, and how her husband Frank killed her in cold blood. Then, after the life was taken away from her helpless body, he turned the gun on himself, falling dead next to her body. Due to Frank's actions, their kids were left without either parent to love and care for them. I just couldn't let that happen to us. Momma, I hope you understand that I just couldn't take that chance! I love my children too much to let that ever happen!

"Besides not wanting myself or my children killed, I also didn't want you to feel the pain of our loss. I can still remember the terrible pain you suffered after Sissy died. I was only five years old when you and daddy brought her home from the hospital. She was my precious baby sister. I was so happy to see her come home after watching her kick inside your stomach for nine months. She was so beautiful. I was finally going to have someone to play with. But after only two months of her arrival, she suddenly died. I heard a lot of people say that she died in her sleep. I heard them call it SIDS. Momma, I'll never forget that day as long as I live. It was also a day we never talked about. A day that died.

"Sissy's death made everyone so sad. I can still remember how you and daddy cried all night long when they took her away from our house. I can also remember how hard it was for you to accept her death. Many years later you still had a hard time coping with her lost. I can remember the many days you wouldn't even get out of bed. Daddy had to help me get off to school. The doctors gave you medication that made you sleep. It was because of her death that you never had any other children. So I knew that if you lost me, your only surviving child and your only grandchildren, you would probably die. So I did what I thought I had to do in order to survive for all of our sakes."

Suddenly Stacy runs into the room. She is scared and crying. Hearing her cries, Gloria immediately puts down the letter and looks up. "Grandma, Grandma. Where are you? Where are you?" Then she spots Gloria and runs toward her.

Gloria holds onto her as tight as she could, assuring her safety. Gloria is puzzled as to why Stacy is afraid. "What is it child? What is it? Grandma's right here." Gloria says as she tried to calm her down. Then she placed Stacy in her lap and holds her close in her arms.

"Grandma, I couldn't sleep. I was having a nightmare about mommy again. I miss her so much. Do you think she'll ever come home and live with us again?" were the cries coming from eight year old Stacy.

Momma, Please Forgive Me!

Gloria knew she had to find a way to assure Stacy that everything would be alright without telling her a lie. "Child, only God knows when your mommy will be coming home. But I'll always be here for you, so don't cry sweetheart." Then Gloria held Stacy close in her arms and rocked back and forth in her rocking chair while calming her down.

Due to Stacy's loud cries, Jr. woke up afraid. "What happened Grandma? Why is Stacy crying? Is she alright? Did she have another one of those bad dreams like mine?"

Gloria was now faced with also easing his concerns. "She's alright. And yes she had one of those dreams. I think I'm going to have to make another appointment with the pastor to help ease both of your fears."

Jr.'s tone became very serious; "Grandma, when people kill other people, do they go to heaven?"

Gloria could not believe his question, but she knew she had to give him a reasonable and honest answer. He was getting old enough to understand the truth. "Well child, sometimes people do go to heaven and sometimes they don't."

Her response scared him. "Grandma, did daddy go to heaven, even though he was mean to mommy?" Just when Gloria thought she had answered the toughest of them all, Jr. had sprung another surprise on her.

Even though Gloria knew that Jonathan's actions were wrong, and she knew that she had no good words to say about him, she respected the fact that he was their father and answered as honestly as she could. "Child, I hope your dad asked God to forgive him. But that is something we'll never know."

Then Stacy looked up at Gloria for answers. "Grandma, even though mommy killed daddy, will she go to heaven when she dies? Does that make her a bad person for what she did to daddy?"

Gloria shook her head, looked up to God for help, took a

deep breathe and answered; "Baby, of course your mommy will go to heaven. I'm sure she didn't mean to kill your daddy. Besides, God forgives anyone who asks for forgiveness. I'm also sure she's asked God to forgive her. So, don't either of you worry about your mommy, she'll be just fine. I'm sure of it."

Then they gave her a big hug and smiled. "Grandma, are you going to heaven when you die?" Stacy asked with curiosity.

Gloria looked at her and smiled. "Of course I am, baby. But I'm not going anytime soon. I'll be right here for a long time to watch over both of you. Now, it's way pass your bedtime. You two need to get some sleep so that you can go to school in the morning. And I promise that Grandma will be right here when you wake up." Then she kissed her grandchildren as they both got down from her lap and ran to the bedroom they shared.

After hearing their cries again, Gloria was beginning to second guess her decision. Originally, she felt that by keeping her grandchildren away from the prison, and away from their mother was the best thing for them. She strongly believed that if La Vonne didn't come home, the kids would one day go on with their lives, putting their mother and the bad experience they endured far behind. Gloria believed that if La Vonne were someday set free, they could then rekindle their long lost relationship and love. But for now, she believed her decision to keep them away was the right thing to do for everyone's sake.

Gloria picks back up her letter and continues reading La Vonne's words; "Momma, I'm sure you're also wondering how I could take the life of another human being after being raised as a Christian. Well, at the time, I thought I was doing the right thing. But now I know that what I did was wrong. I should have gotten help. I should have had the courage to leave. But the look in his eyes grew more fierce each and everyday. Momma, when I saw my baby boy laying on that floor bleeding, I absolutely lost it!

Momma, Please Forgive Me!

It was one thing for him to hit me, but when he hit Jr., anger surfaced like never before. But the last straw was when I noticed the blood streaming down my legs. Momma, this time Jonathan had hit me right in my stomach, killing the unborn twins I was carrying. Then, to make matters even worst, he laughed as he stood there and watched me bleed. He said things like; 'We didn't need no more damn kids around here anyway. I hope the little bastard's die.' Then his laugh got louder. At that very moment I knew that if I hadn't done something quick, none of us would be alive today. Momma, the worst part of losing my precious unborn baby boy's was that I was not able to give them a proper burial. Since I was considered a criminal, the state took them away from me at the hospital and I never knew what happened to their remains. They told me that if I was ever released they would reveal their whereabouts at that time.

"Momma, due to our financial struggles, I was too ashamed to tell you that I was pregnant. So, to tell you that I had also lost the babies was another skeleton I kept to myself. You always stood by daddy's side until the day he died. God bless his soul. Well, I was trying to do the same thing in my marriage. I was trying to be the woman I've always admired in you. Besides, in the beginning of me and Jonathan's relationship, things were great! He loved me and the kids like there was no tomorrow. He was also a very proud man, like daddy was. He worked hard, which allowed me to stay home and raise our kids. Things were very good in the beginning. That's why I loved him so much. But that eventually changed for the worst. I guess now I only have the good times to remember.

"But boy do I remember the good times with dad. I also remember when he died and how hard you took his death. For years you blamed yourself, because it was you who sent him to the grocery store to buy some ice cream. Your sorrowful actions on those special days you and dad shared, shows that you never forgave yourself. You never accepted the fact that someone hit his car and he died on impact. Momma, you have to accept that the accident wasn't your fault. You also have to accept that the things that have happened to me are not your fault. You and daddy raised me the best you knew how, and I love you both for that. You also taught me right from wrong, and even though I did a bad thing, I knew I had to protect myself and my children. I prayed that someday things would get better, but they never did and I was too ashamed to tell you, or ask for your help.

"Momma, I couldn't help the fact that Jonathan followed in the footsteps of his abusive father. Jonathan's mother lived with her husband's abuse all of their life together, until he died of old age. Abuse became something that was considered normal in their household. When I married Jonathan, he vowed to break that cycle, which in the beginning he did. However, after getting involved with the drugs and alcohol, he eventually proved himself a liar, joining the family tradition."

Gloria shook her head in disbelief, put the letter aside, held her head down in her hands and prayed; "Oh Lord God. Where did I go wrong? Lord please forgive her. Please forgive her oh Lord. Also, please help me forgive her as well, as my heart has been hardened by her actions for so long."

Then Gloria picked up the letter and continued reading. "Momma, I know you're crying as you read this letter. I know you don't agree with what I did. Momma, I'm not asking you to agree with me, I'm only asking that you understand why. What I want most from you is to find it in your heart to forgive me. Momma, I also ask that you try to explain to my kids what I did and why. Try to help them understand, as I am still trying to understand myself."

"Momma, help them get on with their lives and not feel guilty for what I did. Tell them that the things that happened to

Momma, Please Forgive Me!

their father was not their fault. Also, tell them that God has forgiven me. Momma, having your forgiveness is all that's left to keep me strong. Your forgiveness will give me the courage to be strong until I come home. I truly believe that being locked away is temporary."

Gloria closed her eyes, held the letter to her heart and thought about La Vonne's words. She knew that somehow she had to forgive her daughter, because she had been taught forgiveness and it was the Christian thing to do. However, the thought of La Vonne killing a human being was something her mind could not envision, even though her heart knew otherwise.

She knew that the only way she was ever going to forgive her daughter was by God's grace. She knew that the Lord needed to open her eyes and allow her heart to do what was right. After reading La Vonne's letter and knowing how bad her grandchildren needed their mother, Gloria knew her heart had to soften.

"Lord, now I understand exactly what La Vonne and my precious grand-babies went through. I can also understand why she kept the things she went through a secret. I've always heard that women of domestic violence avoid the truth and avoid what's real. I understand why La Vonne avoided the truth, which caused her to do something she normally wouldn't have done. I also understand that I must forgive her, or my blessings will continue to be short. I wish she hadn't feared the truth of her marriage by trying to do what was right. I wish she would have left before things got so bad. However, I understand that we can't turn back the hands of time, nor should we judge those who have sinned, for everyone will have to answer to God on judgement day. Lord, I finally accept the forgiveness you are placing inside my heart. I also accept that I could not have prevented my dear husband from leaving this great earth, for his departure time was your will. Lord, I thank you for softening my heart and my will to understand along with my ways of judging others. Whether right or wrong, Lord you have opened my eyes to the truth, the light and the glory in your holy name. You have assured me that everything will someday be alright. Lord, continue to be with us all. Amen." Then Gloria placed the letter on the table and fell fast asleep in her chair.

CHAPTER THREE

It's early in the morning when the loud ringing sound of sirens are heard. La Vonne was locked away in her prison cell, asleep on her hard and cold bed. Her bed was made up with one flattened mattress that rested on an inch thick box spring with a thin blanket for cover. The surprisingly loud sound woke her up, causing her to become frightened. Her curiosity caused her to sit straight up and look around to see what was going on. However, nothing could be seen from her vantage point.

As she looked around, she heard the sounds of several guards speaking through their hand-held radios. Their voices carried loudly throughout the entire building; "There's a fire in dorm number one. Get everybody out of that area immediately! I repeat, there's a fire in dorm number one. All available staff members vacate that area immediately!"

After hearing what was going on, La Vonne jumped out of her bed and put on her clothes as fast as she could. "Oh my God, a fire. Lord, this is the last place where I want to die. Let me hurry up and get ready to get out," she thought while fearing the worst.

Shortly after hearing the voices of the guards, clenching sounds of heavy metal were heard. The guards were opening the cell doors that led to the prison-mates. "Everybody vacate the area quickly. Make a straight line and follow the person ahead of you," one of the guards said loudly. Another guard was leading the group to safety.

Momma, Please Forgive Me!

La Vonne and the other prison-mates walked as fast as they could. They were walking toward the exit that would free them from the dangers of the fire. The outside field was the very yard they mingled with other prison-mates everyday for recreation. This field was the same prison yard that granted their only form of daylight and a somewhat glimpse of the outside world that was hidden over the high brick-wired wall. It was also the same wall that justified freedom. Due to the threatening fire, it was now a place considered as their safety zone.

"Everybody get in your appropriate places now! You know the routine. Get down on the ground!" A guard said with force and authority as he paced back and forth amongst the prisoners. "Put your faces to the dirt and cross your hands over your back. Your hands must be seen at all times. I don't want to see any faces. I only want to see the back of your heads." While he paced, he constantly hit his billy club in the palm of his hand as a warning to those with thoughts of crossing his demands. "If I see anyone's face, all of you will pay dearly!" He said with a very nasty and unpleasant tone.

La Vonne knew from past experiences not to play with any of the guards, especially the men. Many of the male guards had intimating reputations that any woman would fear. Many of their intimidations were forceful and painful, yet pleasurable to their needs. Suddenly, while she laid on the cold dirty field, sounds surfaced through her mind as she began to relive an event that happened the night before, while she was asleep. This event echoed the painful sounds of a prison-mate being raped by a male guard. The victim was hollering and screaming, pleading for the dreadful encounter to come to an end. "Please stop, don't do this to me again. Please stop. I won't tell. Just stop. I promise I won't tell anyone," were her repeated cries.

"Shut up, bitch! Just close your mouth and lay here so I can handle my business, or you'll regret the day you were born," were the sounds of the male guard as he forcefully raped the prison-mate. While La Vonne replayed the sounds of the horrific event and the cries that went unnoticed, she began feeling sick. The sounds of his voice escalated, while playing over and over in her head.

Soon, the reality of this brutal person's voice became clear, it was the same guard who was watching their every move as they laid on the ground. This was also the same guard who had watched La Vonne several times with lustful eyes. She now realized what triggered her reoccurring nightmare of the night she killed her husband.

"I'll sure be glad when I get out of this place" La Vonne thought. "I don't think I can continue being much stronger. I just don't have the strength to continue fighting each and every day. Things have to change. I have to get out of here soon. They're keeping me in here like I'm a criminal, when actually I'm the victim." La Vonne continued her deep thoughts while she patiently waited for the fear of the fire to pass. Due to the lengthiness of the wait, she looked forward in returning to her cell.

After two years of being incarcerated, seeing, hearing and experiencing the brutal sexual violations committed against the prison-mates, in addition to not seeing or hearing from her mother or children, was enough to make anyone want to run. She became more desperate than ever to find a way out.

As she laid on the dirty ground, covered with sand and rocks that were clinging to her face and mouth, she closed her eyes, causing her thoughts of escaping to fully surface. "I wonder if I would have a real chance of escaping. I wonder if I would even make it back home to my mom and kids if I ran. I wonder if I did make it home, if Momma would even take me in, seeing that she's never answered any of my letters or forgiven me for killing Jonathan. I wonder if my children will still love me, knowing that

Momma, Please Forgive Me!

I took their father away from them."

Finally her thoughts were halted as the prison guard gave the command for everyone to stand to their feet. "Everybody get up nice and slow and form a straight line. And don't try anything funny, because I'm too tired today, or I'll have the last laugh." La Vonne frowned. She knew why he was so tired and so did her cell-mate who was grieving in pain from his abuse. Everyone stood to their feet and formed a single file line. They slowly walked toward the building with the guards watching their every move.

After arriving inside of their dorm area, the guards personally escorted each prison-mate back to their individual cell and locked the doors. The loud clinging sound of the metal doors closing were sounds La Vonne never got used to hearing, nor did she ever want to get used to the horrible sound.

Shortly after her door shut, a guard came to her cell and told her that a visitor was waiting to see her in the prisoners meeting room. This visitor was her attorney, Ron Richards, who was a public defender. Ron was a frail and wrinkled white man who was small in stature. His rectangular shaped glasses and narrow-shaped face made him look like a nerd. Due to her no income financial status, Ron had been La Vonne's attorney since she arrived.

Unaware of who her visitor was, La Vonne was more than happy to go to the meeting room. Any chance of getting away from her cell was always welcomed. Oftentimes, her visits were from Pastor George, the minister at her mother's church. Through the years, Pastor George had visited La Vonne on several occasions. Due to his visits, she was able to hold on to the faith of someday returning home to her mother and children. Pastor George was a good man. He always had time for his members. He was a short, brown-skinned man with a balded head. It shinned from the bright lights in the church every time he spoke a sermon. His voice was soft, but his words were always powerful, gaining respect from every person he met.

However, upon her arrival to the meeting room, she became very upset and disappointed to see that it was Ron who was patiently waiting. She had become so accustomed to hearing only bad news from Ron that she didn't welcome his visits; therefore a visit from him was next to nothing. In fact, many times she felt that his visits were as bad as being locked away in her cell.

"Hi, La Vonne, how are you doing?" He said with a big smile on his shinny red face. She looked at him and frowned.; "Why are you here?" she said in a very unpleasant tone. "Is something good going on with my case? Because if you don't have anything good to say, I don't want to hear about it." La Vonne turned away abruptly.

Ron had become accustomed to her somber tone and attempted to ignore it. "As a matter of fact something good is going on with your case." He said happily. Her patience had become short with him, causing her to respond sarcastically; "Well, what is it? Are you going to tell me or not?"

"La Vonne, calm down. I told you that everything would be alright, and today I'm holding up to my promise by letting you know that the judge has granted you an appeal. It's set for later today."

The words coming from his mouth were heavenly to her ears. She suddenly jumped up and down in the air, while wearing a large smile that brightened the entire room. "An appeal date, today! Oh my God, I'm going to finally get out of here! I can't believe it." She looked toward the ceiling, held her hands high in the air: "Thank God, you've finally answered my prayers."

Suddenly Ron's face took a turn in the opposite direction. "Hold on, don't get too excited yet. You still have to talk to the judge and prove that you can cope with the everyday world. Then you have to assure him that you're sorry for your mistakes and that you made a very bad judgement call. Then it's up to him to decide if you're ready to be released or not."

Suddenly a frown appeared on La Vonne's face. She began to stare into Ron's eyes with looks of rage. "It never fails!" she pounded her hand down hard on the small wooden table, causing Ron's glasses to fall down below his lip due to fright. "You're never optimistic about anything! You always want to give me the bad news along with the good. Can't you ever just come in here and tell me the good news and leave the bad news out of the conversation? Since I've been in this dump I've heard enough bad news to last a lifetime." Then she paced back and forth through the small meeting room.

Ron suddenly cleared his voice, put his glasses in place, straightened his posture and attempted to stand his ground in defense of his comments. "La Vonne, as your lawyer I feel that I must tell you the good and bad news of any situation. By doing so, it'll protect you from getting your hopes up too high, only to be brought down harder."

La Vonne looked at him with a very disappointed look on her face, speaking with a calm tone. "Ron, all you ever have to say are the bad things. You never say anything good, and I'm just sick and tired of hearing about all of the bad stuff."

Suddenly her tone changes to cocky. "Ron, as my so-called lawyer I expect for you to come in here and tell me that I'll be free. I need for you to tell me that you're going to make sure I'm freed. I don't want to hear you say that even though I have an appeal I may not get out of this dump. Can't you just come in here with the good news and leave the bad news to yourself sometimes?"

Then her tone changed to somber. "Don't you know that hope is all I have to live on? Don't you know that it's all I have in order to survive in here? No, I guess you wouldn't know or understand anything like that unless you were locked up."

La Vonne was once again very disappointed with the news

from Ron. She shook her head in disbelief. She did not want to hear anything else he had to say. So she called for the guards to let her out. "Guard! Guard! Let me out of here right now!" She said angrily. "I have nothing else to say to this man. Take me back to my cell now!"

Then the guard opened the door and escorted her back to her cell. Ron was left standing alone, shaking his head in disbelief to La Vonne's attitude. He felt bad and pled his case out loud for her to hear. He knew that he had once again let her down. "La Vonne, I'll do everything I can to help you, don't worry. But my hands are tied as to what I'm actually able to do. But don't worry, things will be alright, you'll see." However, his words did not affect her, resulting in her to continue walking, never looking back.

CHAPTER FOUR

The sun of the early dawn is shining on Gloria's country-style home. She had fallen asleep in her rocking chair after reading La Vonne's letter, when suddenly she is awakened by her ten year old grandson. "Grandma, are you awake yet?" Jr. said after trying to softly walk into the livingroom.

Gloria opens her eyes and smiles as she looks at his innocent little face. "Yes, child, I'm awake. How did you sleep last night?"

Jr. smiles back; "I slept good Grandma. I had a good dream last night. Do you want to hear all about it?"

Gloria could see the excitement in his eyes. She sat straight up in her chair and devoted her undivided attention to his words. "Sure I want to hear it. Tell me all about your dream and don't leave anything out." Then he climbed into her lap, hugged her and shared his dream.

Momma, Please Forgive Me!

"Grandma, I dreamed that I was a pilot. I was flying a whole lot of people high in the sky in a real big silver and shiny airplane. Little children would come to me and say 'Hi,' and I would say "Hi," back. They would ask to see inside my airplane and I would let them come in. They would smile when they saw all the things inside the airplane that made it fly. I would tell them that I like to fly and that it was very fun. They would shake my hand and I would shake theirs. Then I would give them some of those plastic wings. They would thank me and smile."

Then his face lit up like the light of the day, causing Gloria to smile as well. "That sounds very interesting. It sounds like you had a very nice dream."

Then he looked up to the ceiling and smiled. "Yeah, it was real nice."

"That's nice." she said as she watched his exciting expressions.

"Grandma, would you fly in my airplane if I did learn how to fly?" He said with a very puzzled look.

Gloria gave him a great big hug and laughed. "Of course I would fly in your airplane. In fact, I would help you fly the airplane if you needed some extra help."

Suddenly his eyes grew as large as saucers with excitement; "You would? Grandma, you would help me fly my big airplane?"

She grinned at his response; "Sure I would if you needed me to."

Jr. gave her a great big hug and together they laughed. Suddenly, his curiosity got the best of him. "Grandma, do you think mommy would fly in my big airplane too?"

She saw the fear that was beginning to creep into his eyes and knew she had to redirect his concerns. "Of course your mommy would fly in your airplane. I'm sure she would fly anywhere you wanted to go."

Then his eyes brighten, as did his expression of excitement. "She would!"

Gloria smiled. She knew she had brightened his mood. "Child, I'm sure your mommy would go anywhere you wanted her to go. In fact, I'm also sure she would help you if you needed extra help as well. So, don't you worry about your mommy. One day she'll be back home to be a part of all your dreams." Then Gloria rocked in her chair as they hugged and smiled.

As Jr. sat in her lap, he thought about La Vonne even more. "Grandma, do you really think mommy will ever come home to live with us again?"

Gloria was amazed by his remarks, but they had become more frequent. "Child, I'm sure she'll come home. I pray to God every night that one day she'll come home soon." Her words again offered encouragement.

"Grandma, when we lived with mommy she used to always tell me that I could be anything I wanted to be when I got older. So, I think that when I get older I'll fly big airplanes high in the sky; then everybody will see my airplane flying and wave at me."

Gloria beamed; "Baby, flying big airplanes sounds like something very nice to do when you get older. Now, it's time for you to get dressed while I fix all of us some breakfast. We can't start our day off right without some of Grandma's good breakfast in our stomachs. So, how does pancakes, bacon, eggs, hashed brown potatoes and orange juice sound to you?"

Jr. jumped down from his grandma's lap, rubbing his stomach. "That sounds good. I'm real hungry now!"

She laughed. "Ok then, go get dressed and tell Stacy to get dressed too."

Then he ran toward the bedroom. "Ok Grandma, I'll tell her. I can't wait to eat. I think all of that dreaming made me extra hungry."

Momma, Please Forgive Me!

After Jr. ran out of the living room, Gloria walked toward the kitchen where she began to quietly pray; "Lord God, please give me the strength to fully forgive La Vonne. Over the last two years my heart has been hardened by what she did. These precious little babies desperately need and miss their mother. I now see that I can't continue keeping them away from her, even if she is in prison. I now know that I have to include Jr. and Stacy in her life. It just isn't fair for me to continue keeping them away from her anymore."

Then Gloria took the letter that she had placed in her bathrobe pocket and continued reading while the children got dressed in their bedroom. "Momma, tell my precious little baby's that I'm sorry for what I did. Tell them that I love them both very much. Tell them that I don't want them to make the same mistakes I made, and that I want them to make me and you both proud. I want them to make better decisions than I made. Also tell them to never let anyone back them in a corner, causing them to make a bad decision like I was forced to make. Momma, I love you and I thank you very much for caring for my baby's while I'm away. I hope to see all of you real soon. Love, La Vonne."

Then Gloria kissed the letter, put it back in her pocket and cried; "La Vonne, I love you too. It's now up to me to make things right. And I have to make things right now!" Then she began to cook their breakfast.

CHAPTER FIVE

La Vonne is now entering the courtroom of appeals. She sees Ron who is smiling at her. She frowns to his gestures, then puts on a happy face in hopes for the best. She is dressed in bright orange colored prison clothes, which are accented with tarnished silver hand and leg cuffs. The added weight of the cuffs make her walk slow. The clinging sounds they are making are drawing the attention of everyone she passes. The guard who has escorted her to court is the same guard who raped her cell-mate the other night. He is also the same guard who frightens many of the prison-mates because they know of his reoccurring actions. His lustful looks make La Vonne very nervous.

As La Vonne slowly makes it to the courtroom table, she takes her seat next to Ron. He whispers in her ear; "La Vonne, things are," she stops him dead in his tracks, whispering louder; "Ron, I don't want to hear anything you have to say. The only thing I want to hear right now is for the judge to announce that I'm free."

Then she put her head down on the cold metal desk and silently prayed. "Lord God, please help me get out of this place. Make things go in my favor. Please release me so that I can go home to be with my children. Thank you Lord." After saying her prayer, La Vonne and Ron waited in silence for the judge to enter the courtroom.

As La Vonne waited, it seemed as if her wait was taking a lifetime. Her thoughts became uneasy and agitated. "Man," she said out loud while hitting her fist on the desk. After realizing how loud her voice was, and the attention she was calling to herself she calmed down, keeping her thoughts to herself. "When is he coming? I'll sure be glad when all of this is over and I'm on my way home. I sure do miss my babies. It would be so nice to see them and momma again." Then she raised her head as the bailiff cleared his throat and spoke. La Vonne is somewhat hopeful, but more unsure because of the pessimistic words Ron spoke the day before.

"All rise for Judge Garret White," the bailiff said with a very authoritative and stern tone in his voice. Judge White takes his seat and everyone sits down. He opens La Vonne's file and begins reviewing it. While reviewing the information, he frowns and shakes his head, gesturing unfavorable movements.

Momma, Please Forgive Me!

As La Vonne watches his expression, she begins to sweat. She becomes very nervous and less confident of being freed. Then he looks up from his rectangular shaped eyeglasses and looks directly at La Vonne with a solemn look on his face. "Ms. Brown, I've reviewed your file. Your case is very interesting. However, before I make my decision, I'd like to hear why you think you should be released."

La Vonne was happy, but nervous by his response. She felt that by him allowing her to voice her opinion she could convince him to free her. She slowly stood up from her chair and addressed his request. Her voice cracked as she spoke; "First of all Your Honor I would like to say that I'm innocent! I did not intentionally kill my husband. I only killed him because I feared for my life and the life of my children. When I looked into his eyes on that dreadful night, I had never seen such rage. All of a sudden he was coming at me so fast I didn't know what to do. He beat me until I bled. Then I bled from the unborn twins I was carrying. At that moment, I knew that if I didn't do something fast to stop his actions I wouldn't be here today to tell my story."

The more she spoke, the more confident she became. Her courage grew stronger in her defense to be freed from prison. "Your Honor, I know that what I did was not the right thing to do, and I'm very sorry. However, during the exact moment of the incident, I believed that killing my husband was the only answer I had left to save my life and the lives of my children. However, after serving over two years in prison, I've changed my mind and I've learned a very hard and serious lesson. I've learned that we shouldn't settle our problems with violence."

Then she cried as she continued; "Your Honor, I also want to say that since I've been incarcerated, I've lived a life of pure hell! Throughout my adult entire life I have endured several beatings and since I've been here I've experienced rape. Now, my body has been bruised for life. I know that this isn't an excuse for what I did, but being incarcerated has taught me to be stronger. It's taught me to think before I react, otherwise the consequences can be overwhelming and unbearable. I beg of you to see it in your heart to release me, as I am not a criminal. My guilt is that I was an abused victim who cried out for help, but help was never there for me. I am also guilty because I didn't search hard enough for a way out. Prison is a place I would never want anyone to become familiar with, let alone my children. I now know that if I'm ever put in a position like that again, and I pray that I'm not, I'll never make the same decision. I'll make sure my choice is smarter and wiser, avoiding the consequences I'm now faced with, along with wearing the blood of another human being for the rest of my life."

La Vonne became restless and sad as she pled her case. Sharing her story brought back all the bad memories of how things were and what she went through. However, she knew that she had to continue with her story in order to prove to the judge that she had changed and was ready to be set free.

"Your Honor, there's no way in God's holy name that I'll ever make the same kind of decision again. Please see it in your heart to forgive me, as God has forgiven me of my sins. Your Honor, I pray that you will release me so that I can go back home and raise my children to do the right things in life. I also hope that you release me so that I can be the best mother I know that I can be. Thank you for hearing my plea." Then La Vonne stood in silence and waited for the judge's instructions.

As she stood there, the judge put his head down and looked over her file once again. Then, in a stern voice he spoke; "Ms. Brown, I've reviewed your file and heard your story. But I'll need more time before I make my final decision. I release you back into the custody of the guard who will return you to your prison cell until I've made my final decision."

Momma, Please Forgive Me!

Then he stood to his feet, picked up the file and walked out of the courtroom and into his chambers. La Vonne was left standing, feeling sad. She felt that the judge had not totally accepted her plea. She was now beginning to realize that her entire life would be spent in prison.

Then the guard walked over and escorted her back to her cell as tears slowly rolled down her face. She looked at Ron and rolled her eyes at him as she was lead away. Ron stood in silence as he watched her walk away, while the clinging sounds of the handcuffs followed her every move.

After reaching her cell, the guard removed her handcuffs. Then he looks at her and smiles. He has a very sarcastic look on his face. "Maybe next time honey." La Vonne looked at him with rage. Then she turned her head and quickly ran toward the back of her cell and laid down on her bed. He locked the door and blew her a kiss and smiled even more. His gesture made her angry, causing her to cry. She prayed to God for the answers and strength she needed to continue to survive as a prisoner in a place she would never call home.

CHAPTER SIX

It's mid afternoon and Gloria has arrived at Ron Richards law office. She has finally forgiven La Vonne. She is ready to help her daughter get out of prison. She feels that with her help, La Vonne may have a better chance of becoming free. "Hello, can I help you?" Ron's secretary said as Gloria walks through the glass double doors. "Yes, you can. I need to see Mr. Ron Richards immediately." Gloria responds with a very demanding tone in her voice.

The secretary is taken by surprise by Gloria's tone. She

looks at Gloria with a puzzled look on her face, wondering what her problem was. "Miss, do you have an appointment with Mr. Richards?"

Suddenly Gloria's tone changes to somber and tears fall from her eyes. "Within the last two years I've had several appointments with Mr. Richards, but I couldn't make any of them. So, now I'm here to makeup for those unkept appointments."

Gloria's statement overwhelmed the secretary, causing her to feel bad. She now wanted to help and gave her tissue. "Miss, what's your name?"

"Gloria Johnson," she said with dignity as she stood poised, proud, straight and tall.

"Thank you Miss Johnson. Have a seat over there and I'll see if Mr. Richards is available. Just one moment please."

Gloria walks toward the chair while wiping the tears away from her eyes. "Thank you."

After Gloria sat down, the secretary called Ron on her telephone. She kept her voice to a whisper so that Gloria could not hear their conversation. "Excuse me, Ron, but a Miss Gloria Johnson is here to see you. She says that she's missed several appointments with you during the last two years. She's also crying. I think you should speak to her right away. She sounds like she really needs your help. Should I send her in now?"

Ron was confused; "Gloria Johnson? I can't remember making any appointments with a Gloria Johnson. Did she say why she needs to see me?"

The secretary looked at Gloria who was still crying and felt really bad for her. "No she didn't, but Ron you should really speak to her, she can't stop crying."

"Ok, send her in."

Then the secretary hung up the telephone and walked toward Gloria. "Excuse me Miss Johnson, Mr. Richards can see you now. Right this way please." Then she walked Gloria down a long hallway and lead her directly to Ron's office.

"Hello," Ron said as he stood from his chair and extended his hand to shake hers. "Please, have a seat." He said as he directed her to sit in the small brown colored plaid chair. "My name is Ron Richards. How may I help you?"

Gloria got comfortable in her chair and looked directly at Ron with her sad and teary eyes; "Hi, I'm La Vonne Brown's mother."

Suddenly Ron knew who she was. "Oh yeah, it's nice to finally meet you Miss Johnson."

Gloria wiped her eyes. "I'm sorry I never made any of your appointments or accepted any of your calls, but at the time I wasn't ready to deal with my daughter's situation. But after a lot of soul searching and praying, I'm ready to help. Is there anything I can do to get my daughter released from prison? Anything at all, just say the word?" Then she blew her nose with the moistened tissue in her hand.

Ron gave her a few fresh sheets of tissue from his box. He knew he had made several unsuccessful attempts to reach her. He wondered why she was ready to help now. "Well, Miss Johnson, right now there's really nothing you can do. In fact, just this morning La Vonne was finally granted a hearing from an appeal's judge. That's quite an accomplishment, because it often takes a long time to get an appeal hearing. She's been waiting for this day for the past two years. So at least things are finally moving forward."

Gloria felt hopeful. "Oh, thank God. Lord, thank you!" She said as she raised her hands high above her head, looking toward the ceiling. "So, now what Mr. Richards?"

Ron was enjoying her excitement. "Call me Ron, Mr. Richards is so formal."

"Ok Ron. Now what happens?"

"Anyway Gloria." Ron hastily said, causing Gloria to look at him with shock on her face.

"It's Miss Johnson, thank you," she said in a nasty tone, demanding respect.

Ron cleared his throat from his embarrassment and continued; "Excuse me, Miss Johnson. Like I was about to say, the judge has heard your daughters appeal. By the way, La Vonne did an excellent job of pleading her case. But I do have to warn you to not get your hopes up too high. You see anything can happen when it comes to dealing with a judge. Nothing is for sure."

Gloria's hopes become uncertain. "So what happens now? Does she gets out of prison or not?" Then she looked at Ron with a very serious look on her face.

He looked at her with a very unsure look on his; "Well, we'll just have to wait and see what happens now. After the judge has fully examined La Vonne's case, he'll notify us and give us his final verdict. Hopefully he'll realize that she's not a criminal, and only a mother who was trying to protect herself and her children, even if her actions were not the right thing to do."

Gloria wasn't sure how to take his news. However, she did know that she had a higher authority that could make a way. "Mr. Richards, I mean Ron, there's no hope about any of this. It's all about having faith and praying for what you need. And right now, it seems that the only way La Vonne will ever see the outside of those prison walls is through prayer."

Ron shook his head in agreement. "You said the magic word, prayer. Because with all of the facts against your daughter, it will take some form of a higher power to get her released right now. If she wouldn't have shot him while he laid asleep, or if there had been a struggle between them when the gun went off, she would have had a better chance of being set free. In fact, she may have even went home the very night the incident, but that wasn't the case. Therefore, proving her incidence is harder. From a legal prospective your daughter had a well planned motive to kill her husband, and not just a plan to defend herself and her children. So, I'll be really surprised if she's set free. However, like you said, God can do all. I also think that your daughter has a very good chance of being released because of her testimony. She spoke very well and if the judge sympathies with her motive, she should be home by tomorrow."

Suddenly Gloria's mood changed, causing her eyes to light the room. "You do? I agree, my daughter is no criminal! She was only doing what she thought was the right thing to do. I'm sure God has forgiven her of her sins, because he taught me how to forgive."

Ron shook his head and smiled. "Miss Johnson, as far as I see it, I truly believe that when the judge realizes that La Vonne made several attempts to get help from the police, and they never responded, says a whole lot on her behalf."

"You think so?" Gloria said with little confidence as Ron continued.

"Miss Johnson, your daughter has been a model prisoner she's been incarcerated. That also adds a lot to her case. But again, we must not jump the gun. We have to wait for the judge's verdict. Lets face it, thirty years to life is a long time for anyone to stay locked up for defending their own life."

Gloria agreed and cried; "All I ever wanted, was for my daughter and grandchildren to be happy. She's the only daughter I have. I had no idea what kind of pain they were living with each and every day. My daughter never mentioned that anything was wrong. She always told me that everything was all right. I guess her pride got in the way of her doing what was right. If I would have only known sooner, none of this would have ever happened." Then she wiped away more tears.

Ron felt sorry for her and tried to offer comforting words. "Miss Johnson, you can't blame yourself for any of this, you didn't know. You also can't turn back the hands of time. The only thing you can do is be there for your daughter, no matter what happens."

Suddenly Gloria regained her composure and felt her strength resurfacing. "Ron, you can definitely count on!" Then they smiled.

Gloria stood up and extended her hand to Ron. "Well, I've taken up enough of your time. Thank you for seeing me with no appointment. It's now time for me to go home and do some serious praying for my daughter, she'll need them."

"She sure will," Ron said while walking her toward the door. "Miss Johnson, I'll keep you posted with any news on your daughter's case. Thank you for coming in, come anytime."

Gloria smiled and shook her head. "Thank you for sticking with my daughter through this trying time. I'll be in touch. Goodbye." Then she walked out the door.

"I'll look forward in hearing from you." Ron said as she left his office.

CHAPTER SEVEN

It's late in the afternoon at Gloria's house. As she walks into the door, Jr. runs into her arms; "Hi Grandma!"

She sees the joy in his eyes, smiles and gives him a big bear hug. "Hi, sweetheart."

He's surprised as to why she's been gone all afternoon. "Grandma, where'd you go?"

Knowing how curious Jr. is, she knew the questions were just beginning. "Sweetheart, Grandma had some business to take care of." Gloria begins looking through her mail she brought into the house.

Of course his curiosity was getting the best of him with her vague answer. "What kind of business?" He said with a puzzled look on his face.

Suddenly, Gloria's voice developed a sarcastic tone, which was a sign that this was her last answer to his question. "Grown folks business," she said, as he looked at her with shock. "I was taking care of grown folks' business, that's what kind of business I was taking care of." Jr. knew from her words and expression that the question and answer session was now over, causing him to quietly return to his room.

Gloria begins her conversation with Rae, the lady who lives next door that was watching the kids while she was gone. "Thanks Rae for watching the kids. I can handle things from here. You can go home now."

Rae gathered her belongings that were laying on the couch. "No problem Gloria, you take care. Bye."

Gloria waved as Rae walked out the door. "You do the same, bye." Then she closed the door and went into her bedroom to change her clothes so that she could prepare dinner.

The children were in their room playing quietly. Gloria was now in the kitchen cooking, thinking about her day. "I wonder if things will work out for La Vonne. God knows that I love that child. I sure hope the judge sees things God's way and releases her. Just think, if he does, she'll be home in time for the thanksgiving holiday next month. I'm sure she'd appreciate a full turkey dinner with all the extra's after eating prison food for two years. La Vonne has always loved my turkey dinners served with cornbread dressing, black-eyed-peas, collar greens, yams, macaroni and cheese, mashed potatoes, cranberry sauce, a tossed salad, hot buttered rolls, sweet potato pie and peach cobbler. Umm, I'm getting hungry just thinking about it. There's nothing like a good home cooked meal."

Then Gloria continued warming up her yesterday's leftovers which included macaroni and cheese, honey-baked ham, fresh picked string beans from her garden and fresh banana pie for her and her grandchildren.

CHAPTER EIGHT

It's late at night in the prison where La Vonne now realized, but didn't accept as her home. Everyone was sleep. The entire prison dorm was free from sound, when suddenly La Vonne was awakened. Someone was invading her privacy. "Get out of here! I mean it, both of you get out of here right now or I'll scream," she said to the intruders with fear layered throughout her voice.

"Go ahead bitch, scream all you want. But if you do, it'll be the last scream anyone will hear from you. You'll pay extra for any screams heard." One of the female prison-mates said after a guard had allowed her and another prison-mate to enter La Vonne's locked cell.

La Vonne knew from past experiences that they meant every threat they made, because raping other prison-mates was something these two did often, which they highly enjoyed. La Vonne knew that she had to remain quiet and hope that they quickly left. But tonight was not her lucky night, in fact tonight would be a night she feared most. It would be a night she would forever remember with pain and humiliation.

They turned her on her back and viciously raped her with the handle of a broken broom stick, along with their bare hands. As she laid there trying not to scream, La Vonne silently cried and prayed for them to stop. "Lord God, please help me! Please make them stop! Please Lord, make them stop right now! They're going to kill me if they keep this up. Right now dying would feel better than the way they're making me feel." Through her agony and pain, La Vonne continued to pray in order to gain the needed strength as thoughts flooded her mind.

"I can't allow anyone to ever bring me down like this again! So Lord, please make them stop! I know you say that you will only give us what we can bear, but Lord this is definitely unbearable. I'm not this strong! Lord you also said that there is a good lesson to be learned from every bad experience. Well, the only lesson I can see coming from this experience of pain and humiliation can only do one thing for me, make me stronger. I have to be strong in order to survive. I must stay strong for my children. I'm not giving up on being set free, or free from their abuse. I have to do what I need to do in order to prevent this from ever happening again. From this day on, nothing like this will ever happen to me! Also from this day on, I promise that this will be the very last time I cry. Because, after an experience like this, I can be strong amoungst the greatest of pain. The next time I will ever cry will be the day I'm set free!" Then she continued to silently cry as they enjoyed the pleasure of sex and power forced to her body, while she suffered with the pain.

Suddenly a sound was heard in the prison area where they were located, causing the women to get off La Vonne and run out of her cell. After they left, the door was slightly opened. La Vonne went to the door and closed it as much as she could without the key to lock it shut. She used one of her bows from her hair to tie the door closed. Then she went back to her bed and positioned herself in a ball, like a newborn baby and rocked back and forth, silently praying repeatedly until she fell asleep. "Thank you God. Oh thank you God that it's over! Thank you God. Oh thank you God!"

****

It was finally daylight. The early hours of the sun-rising

morning became La Vonne's savor. Since she had been incarcerated, none of the horrific events seemed to happen during daylight. Daylight was something she longed for during several frightening nights. Daylight became her friend and her safety zone.

Everyone was getting up and attending to their daily duties. La Vonne was still laying in her bed. Due to the pain she was still feeling from her terrifying even, she could hardly move. She figured that if she just laid there quietly, no one would realize that she was not attending her duties.

"Wake up missy." One of the guards said who came to her cell door. "You have a visitor waiting to see you. So hurry up and get dressed. You don't want to keep any visitors waiting, do you? Those are the only sources to the real world you have. So hurry up so I can take my break and get something to eat."

Then the guard moved away from the door and La Vonne got dressed, un-tied the bow off of the cell door and walked out of her unlocked room to meet the guard. "I'm ready." She said as he put on her handcuffs and she slowly walked away.

After reaching the meeting room, La Vonne was disappointed to find Ron standing there smiling. "Hi, La Vonne, how are you doing? He said as he extended his hand out for her to shake. With an upsetting look on her face, she ignored his gesture and carefully sat down. Then as she watched him smile so pleasantly, she snapped, roaring at his greeting; "How would you be doing if you just got fucked in your ass?"

Her words were so forceful and frightening that Ron became speechless. She had caught him off guard. "I'm sorry. I didn't know."

Then La Vonne continued her roar; "Of course you didn't know. In fact, you'll probably never know because you'll probably never live in prison. I guess when you're white, and born with a silver spoon in your mouth, something like this would be hard to

Momma, Please Forgive Me!

imagine. Now tell me, Ron, how can you know anything about being raped if you've never experienced the act personally? Do you think its been fun and games living here? Or maybe that everything is going alright and we're all just one big happy family in this hell hole? And don't say that you feel sorry for me. Just get me the hell out of here fast! If the judge would have released me yesterday, none of this would have ever happened. Now, I'm scarred again for life!" She put her head down on the table and held back her tears, rocking her head back and forth in disgust.

Ron's facial expressions showed that he was totally startled. He had never seen her react quite this way before. He didn't know whether to fear for his life or feel sorry for her. He definitely didn't want to be in her shoes. He knew deep down inside that he was limited as to what he could do, and he didn't feel very optimistic about La Vonne being set free. "I'm sorry, La Vonne. I'm really sorry. Is there anything I can do to help?"

She looked at him with blood in her eyes and screamed as loud as she could. "I said that you could get me out of this hell hole, that's what you can do for me! That's all you can do for me! Do you get that?"

Ron jumped with fear as her rage was directed at him. He knew that he had to again prove his point. "La Vonne, I need for you to bear with me. I'm trying to do all I can. But I can't do it alone."

"Bear with you? Bear with you?" La Vonne said with fury. "How in the hell can you ask me to bear with you after what I've been through? I've been through some major shit since I've been here, but never anything like this. And this pain could have been spared if the damn judge would have just released me yesterday. But no, he had to review my files some more. Hell, he should have reviewed them before he came to court. Am I ever going to get out of this place or what?"

Ron really became scared as he watched her anger rise. "I know being patient is a bit much for me to ask of you, but everything is in the judges hand, not mine. I can only do so much, I'm sorry." Then he held his head down and frowned.

La Vonne could see the uneasiness and lack of confidence displayed in Ron's face which made her break down in sorrow. She felt that he was her last hope to help her become free. Feeling sorry for her just wasn't good enough anymore. Becoming free was all she wanted to hear. "There you go feeling sorry again. Do me a favor and don't! Just get me the fuck out of here, that's all I ask of you, is to just get me out of here! Besides, you said that you've always felt that I got the short end of the stick, so why is it so hard for me to become free? I just have to get out of this hell hole or I'll lose my mind or get killed. I can't keep taking this kind of treatment. I gotta get out of here now! Exactly, why are you here anyway?" La Vonne's mood suddenly changed. She had voiced her point of view, blew off a lot of steam and was now ready to hear what he had to say.

Ron cleared his voice; "Well, with all you've been though, I almost forgot what I came here to tell you. Oh yeah, I remember now. Anyway, I came here to tell you that I got a visit from your mother."

La Vonne's mouth dropped with excitement. "My mom? My mom came to see you?"

Then Ron continued; "She misses you very much and wants you to come home."

La Vonne forgot about her pain and stood to her feet and jumped up and down in place. "I can't believe that after two long years momma came to see you. She must have finally read my letter. What did she say? Does she forgive me? How are my kids doing? Did they come with her?" The questions were coming out of La Vonne's mouth so fast that Ron couldn't keep up with all of

Momma, Please Forgive Me!

them. He enjoyed watching her joy. Her joy made the visit worthwhile, especially after the way it began.

"Calm down. Calm down. One question at a time is all I can answer. No, the kids didn't come with her. But I'm sure they're fine because she didn't mention that anything was wrong. And yes, I'm sure she forgives you, because she said that she should have come to see me much sooner. She said that in the beginning, she couldn't handle your situation, but now she can. The main thing she wanted to know was if she could help get you released."

"Yes, yes, yes!" La Vonne happily said as she listened to the good news. "I knew she'd come around. I just knew she would. Well, can she help? Can she? Is there anything she can do to help get me out of here? Maybe she can talk to the judge. Maybe if he listens to her, I'll get out for sure. Maybe now that she wants to help, my chances of getting out are better, especially since God is really on her side."

Ron was enjoying the excitement coming from La Vonne. This excitement was something he had never seen during the entire two years she had been incarcerated. Today was definitely one of those rare and unusual days on both extremes. "Well that's exactly what I told her was to pray. But wait, I have more good news."

La Vonne looked at him with such excitement on her face that she could hardly contain her emotions. "More good news? Well, what else happened? What? Tell me!"

"After your mother left my office, I called the judge's office to see when we could possibly expect to hear his decision."

La Vonne was almost dancing from all of the excitement. "Well, hurry up and tell me. What did they say? Can I get out now? Did he grant my appeal? Tell me! Tell me!"

Ron shook his head and smiled. "Slow down. Slow down."
"I can't slow down. Tell me now!"

Ron was now smiling from ear to ear as a result of her excitement. "They told me that he would be ready to give us his decision tomorrow morning."

"Tomorrow? Why didn't you tell me all this good news when you first walked in? Thank God! Tonight will be my last night in this hell hole."

Abruptly Ron changed the mood. "Calm down. Don't count your chickens before they hatch."

La Vonne looked at him with a very disturbed look on her face and sat down to take the full blow of his delivery. "Why?"

After all the celebrating, Ron had to put it all to an end by revealing reality. "Because the judge can rule either way, we don't know if he thinks you're ready to get out or not. So it's best to not get too excited, just in case."

La Vonne's good mood was now lost. "There you go again. Mr. Pessimistic! Ron tell me something, why is it that you always have to burst my bubble? Especially when everything was going so well? Why couldn't you just let bygones be bygones? Why couldn't you have left the decision of the judge, up to the judge and not include your two cents? Why do you always have to give your so-called point-of-view? What should I have expected anyway? I guess I should have figured that you would find some way to bring me down. You've been the same way for the last two years, so why should I have expected anything different now?"

Ron put his head down and scratched the bald spot on the top of his head. "La Vonne, I'm not trying to burst your bubble. I'm only trying to tell you the truth so that your bubble doesn't get burst while you're standing in front of the judge." He said as his voiced cracked from lack of confidence.

La Vonne became cocky; "Isn't that just nice! You don't want to burst my bubble. You know that I shouldn't be in this damn place anyway!" Knowing that he was her only way to gain

Momma, Please Forgive Me!

freedom, La Vonne tried a softer approach with Ron. "You're my lawyer. You're supposed to believe in me, not just wait to see what the judge has to say. Why can't you give me some kind of hope and faith? I can't keep living my life with little or no hope. I can't keep living like this. I'll die in here if I don't get out soon, last night is proof of that. Please Ron, I beg of you to get me out of here. Try to pull some kind of strings somewhere, somehow! But please don't let me spend another night in this place!" Then La Vonne walked toward the door to signal for the guard to escort her back to her cell.

Ron packed his briefcase, knowing that by doing his job he had again let her down. "La Vonne, I'm sorry I couldn't be more positive. But I have to be truthful and honest with you. It's not just my job, it's what I believe in."

Suddenly La Vonne looked at Ron with a look that would surely kill. "Ron, if the judge denies my release, do me a favor and don't come back! Because if you can't say anything positive about my case and work harder to get me out of here, then I don't need you. So don't come back if my appeal is denied." Then the guard lead her out of the meeting room and back to her cell. Ron was left standing alone, feeling helpless, scratching his bald head.

CHAPTER NINE

It's five in the morning and Gloria is asleep in her bed. The house is totally dark when Jr. abruptly runs toward her room crying. "Grandma, Grandma. Where are you? Where are you Grandma," he cries in a panic. Due to his cries, Gloria becomes frightened and immediately wakes up and attempts to run toward him when he meets her at her bed. "Grandma's right here! What's the matter baby? Tell Grandma what's the matter?"

Jr. jumps in her bed and holds her as tight as he could. He can not control his crying. "Grandma, I had another bad dream." After hearing his explanation Gloria is not surprised. "The one with your dad hitting your mom?" she said while rocking him in her arms, where his head rested under her bosom. "Yes Grandma, that's the one. Grandma make it stop. Please make the bad dreams stop!" Then he continued crying.

"Oh baby, it's alright. Your daddy will never be able to hurt your mommy again. Try not to think about it, it's over now! Grandma's here to protect you. Grandma's not going to let anybody hurt you. Everything will be alright I promise, ok." Suddenly he felt better. "Ok Grandma, I'll try." Then she kissed him on his forehead and squeezed him tighter.
"Do you feel better now?"
He looks at her and smiles. "Yes."

After an hour of talking and rocking, they both smile, feeling relived and comforted. Gloria feels better knowing that she has eased his fears. "That's my little man. So, now that you feel better, go get dressed. It's time for you and Stacy to get ready for school now. Grandma will make you both a nice big breakfast. I bet a nice big breakfast will make you feel better, won't it?" They both look at each other and smile. "Yes it would." Then he jumped out of Gloria's lap and went to get dressed. Gloria fixed the kids a big breakfast and things were back to normal, just like nothing had ever happened.

As the day went on, the afternoon was sunny and beautiful. The kids had come home from school and were in their bedroom playing.

Gloria was in the livingroom watching television. "Grandma, can I go outside and play?" Stacy said. Gloria looks at the excitement in the eyes of her eight year old granddaughter and

Momma, Please Forgive Me!

grins. Then Jr. follows behind; "Me too Grandma. Can I go too?" They both jump up and down, waiting for Gloria's response.

"Sure you can, but make sure your room is clean." She says as they run toward their room to look.

"Mine is clean." Stacy says.

"Mine too Grandma." Jr. repeats.

Gloria shakes her head and smiles; "Ok, you can go, but don't go too far." She warns them. "I want both of you to stay right in front of this house. Do you hear me?" she said with authority. "We hear you Grandma. We'll stay right here, bye." They both said in unison as they quickly ran out the door.

After they left, the telephone rang. Gloria got out of her favorite chair to answer; "Hello," she said.

"Hello, is this Miss Johnson?" The mystery caller politely said.

"Yes, this is she? Who am I speaking too?" Gloria curiously said.

"Hi Miss Johnson, this is Ron Richards, La Vonne's lawyer."

"Yes Mr. Richards, I mean Ron. What can I do for you today? Is La Vonne alright? Did the judge make his decision yet?"

Ron smiled. He now knew where La Vonne got her impatient personality from. "Slow down Miss Johnson. Yes, everything is alright. So far the judge has not made his decision yet. However, he will be making it tomorrow morning. That's why I'm calling. If you'd like, you can come to the courtroom and hear what the judge has to say yourself. How does that sound?"

Gloria became totally elated. "Oh yes! I would love to come. I've forgiven La Vonne and now I need to let her know that I've forgiven her personally. Right now I just want to see her free. I want for her to come home and raise her children, they need her so bad. So tell me, what time and where do I need to go?" Then she got a pencil and paper and wrote down the instructions. Ron felt good that he made her happy, in spite of the way he made La Vonne feel earlier.

CHAPTER TEN

The next morning has finally come. Due to the excitement of seeing La Vonne, along with the possibilities of her actually coming home, Gloria was barely able to sleep. She is so nervous and excited that she can't seem to find the things she needs to get ready. "Oh my God, today may be the day La Vonne comes home. Where are my stockings? I just had them." Gloria says as she hurries to get dressed.

Earlier, she had called some of her friends after speaking with Ron about going with her to the courtroom. Gloria has not told her grandchildren about the news. She feels it would be better for La Vonne to just come home and surprise them, rather than breaking their hearts if the judge doesn't grant her appeal. "Now, I'm ready." She says after taking that last look in the full length mirror behind the bathroom door. Gloria then gets in her car and goes to pick up three of her church friends, Gina, Susan and Nancy, and they all go to the courtroom.

As she walks into the prison area, Gloria becomes nervous. Her friends are equally nervous. None of them are used to the surroundings, along with the procedures needed in order to enter. This is their first visit to the prison. As they follow the entering procedures of going through the metal detector and having their handbags x-rayed for prohibited items, they see many prison-guards patrolling the building. They also notice a few prisoners who are being escorted by various guards to various locations. The sight of all the security guards and prisoners cause them to walk closer together with their arms locked tight. Their eyes are focused on every movement and their reactions are very fearful.

They finally reach the courtroom where La Vonne's appeal will take place and have a seat together. "Thank God we finally made it here." Gloria nervously said as she held the hands of two of the women seated next to her. "Thank God you guys came with me. I don't know what I would have done if I had to come alone." Gloria whispered. Then they all sat in silence, looked around cautiously and waited for the procedures to begin.

Shortly after, La Vonne walked into the courtroom wearing brightly colored orange prison clothes, along with leg and arm chains and cuffs. Again, the sound of the cuffs drew everyone's attention. At the very site of La Vonne, Gloria cried. She was trying to hold back her tears and keep her cries to herself, but she couldn't. Her friends immediately pulled tissue out of their purses, giving some to Gloria and keeping some for themselves. The sounds of Gloria crying drew the attention of La Vonne, who smiled, held back her tears and waved.

After Gloria saw the sad look on her daughter's face, she stood straight up in her seat and called out; "My baby! Look at my baby!" A guard quickly walked toward Gloria in an effort to calm her down. "Excuse me Miss, but you're going to have to keep the noise down and stay in your seat. Otherwise, you'll be asked to leave the courtroom." Gloria looked at the guard, turned her nose up to him and quietly sat down, wiping away the tears from her face with her tissue.

La Vonne sees the guard's action and sits down, not saying a word. She did not want the guard to escort her mother out of the courtroom. After La Vonne is seated, she smiles and looks back, speaking in a whisper; "Hi Momma, glad you could come."

Then they both reached toward each other and smiled. Gloria blew La Vonne a kiss which made her happy. La Vonne's true feelings were halted, due to being locked up and closely watched by a guard. The bailiff stands to his feet and with a loud and firm tone announced the judge's arrival. "All rise for Judge Garret White."

Everyone in the courtroom stood to their feet. "Please be seated now." The bailiff said after the judge took his seat. Then the judge spoke; "Ms. La Vonne Brown, please rise." La Vonne slowly and nervously stood to her feet. She was ready to hear the judge's verdict, while hoping for the best.

In a very forceful and intimidating tone, the judge spoke; "Ms. Brown, I've reviewed your case and heard your plea. I'm now ready to give my decision." His tone frightened her, causing her to come to the conclusion that she would not be released. However, she held on to hope and her prayers as the judge continued.

"Ms. Brown, I know you believe that you're the victim, but you're not! Mr. Brown is the victim because you killed him in cold blood while he slept on the couch of your livingroom. Those actions do not validate self defense, only murder! Ms. Brown, I truly feel sorry that this kind of abuse was administered to you by your husband over the years. However, that does not excuse you from what you did. We can not go around in society killing everyone who hurts us. We have to put crime in the hands of the law, even when it seems that the law isn't always fair. We still can't take things into our own hands. Ms. Brown, at this time I can not grant your release, I'm sorry. Court is dismissed."

Then the judge hit his gavel on the table, stood up from his chair, gathered his belongings and went to his private chambers, firmly closing the door behind him.

As he is leaving La Vonne begins to holler and scream hysterically; "No! No!!! You can't send me back there, you just can't! Please judge, come back! Please don't make me go back

Momma, Please Forgive Me!

there! Please, come back!" She roared hysterically, while keeping her promise of not crying. However, the judge had disappeared out of sight. La Vonne was so mad that the guards had to contain her in her seat, until she calmed down.

As La Vonne begged for mercy, Gloria cried and ran to be at La Vonne's side. La Vonne's lawyer looked at the guard and approved the exchange of hugs while everyone looked on and cried. As Gloria held her daughter as tight as she could, her cries become louder; "It's gonna be alright, I promise. I'm here now to help you. I'll do everything I can in order to get you out of here."

La Vonne's eyes were filling with water, however she refused to cry. "Thank you Momma. It's so good to see you. It's been a long time." She joyfully said as they hugged. "Well, that won't happen again. I'm here now and I'm here to help you." Gloria said as their hug continued.

"Momma, how are my precious little babies doing?" La Vonne said with excitement and curiosity. "They're doing just fine, just fine baby. They miss you very much." Gloria said with sadness.

"I miss them too." La Vonne was still trying to not cry. "Momma, tell them I love them very much and that I want to see them real soon."
"Don't worry, I'll tell them for you."

After Gloria and La Vonne finally let go of each other, La Vonne looked at Ron with hate in her eyes and anger in her voice. "Ron, you're fired! Get out of here right now! Over the last two years all you've ever done was give me excuses. If you were doing your job correctly I would have been out of here a long time ago. So go, just leave! I don't need you anymore. My mother is here to help me now and I don't need you ever again!"

Ron was left standing there in shock, scratching his bald head. After hearing La Vonne's harsh words, he did not know what to do or how to react. "I'm sorry La Vonne. I tried to help you, but your case was just too tough."

La Vonne couldn't believe his words. "Too tough? You just didn't know what you were doing. I guess that's what I get for not having enough money to pay for a decent defense lawyer. The poor people are always the ones who have to pay with their lives and with their souls. Just like I paid a high price with all those beatings I got from my so-called victimized husband. If the police would have come to my defense when I called on them the first time, I wouldn't be spending my life in this hell hole right now! I'd be at home raising my children, myself!"

Everyone in the entire room was stunned by La Vonne's behavior, but she wouldn't let anyone get a word in to aid Ron's defense. The guards just stood back with their arms folded and enjoyed the excitement as she continued; "I guess if I were white like you and lived in a fancy house, none of this would have ever happened in the first place! I guess that's the price you pay for being poor, black and a woman. I bet if my husband had reported that I was beating him the police would have come running faster than anyone could have counted to three. But when a woman calls for help, no one is there to help, until it's too late. I sure hope that one day the police will come when a woman calls for help. It's a damn shame that in 1990 domestic violence is still an unimportant issue to many. Maybe if a white woman gets killed by a black man, the laws will change! But only then will things change!"

La Vonne finally halted her rage. Her anger had allowed her to work herself up to the point of danger. As she stood there looking at Ron with rage, her heart was racing. Her heavy breathing became very noticeable to everyone in the room, resulting in them trying to calm her down.

Gloria was more shocked than Ron. It had been over two years since she'd communicated with her daughter and was not

Momma, Please Forgive Me!

prepared for the anger she was hearing. "La Vonne, calm down honey. I've never seen you act like this. I know you're mad, but you can't take it out on Ron. He was only doing his job."

La Vonne looked at her mom, then at Ron who had been silent the entire time. "That's the point Momma, he was ONLY doing his job. And if I had money to pay him, his job would have been done a whole lot better. So no, I don't need him as my lawyer anymore. I can do bad all by myself. I don't need him. Over the last two years he's only told me what can't happen with my case, and what he couldn't do to help me. So Mr. Richards, like I said earlier, you can leave. I don't need you in my life ever again! You've wasted enough of my time as it is. I could have defended myself better than what you've done, and you call yourself a lawyer. Well, if that's your title, they need to give you a new one. Because I thought a lawyer defends their clients, not tells them what he can't do for them."

Ron's red face was furious. He packed up his briefcase and quickly stormed out of the courtroom feeling embarrassed. The guard decided that the show was now over and it was time for La Vonne to return to what was her home, prison. "La Vonne, it's time to go now."

Gloria tried to keep her there a little longer; "Wait, don't take her now. I haven't seen her in over two years. I'm not ready to say goodbye yet." The guard looked at Gloria and escorted La Vonne toward the exit door. "I'm sorry Miss, but I have to take her back to her cell now or I'll be in trouble. We've already let her stay longer than we were supposed to let her stay. You can come back tomorrow, during visiting hours."

Gloria gave La Vonne one last hug before she left. After hearing the unpleasant news, La Vonne was just thankful that her mother had finally come around and was now going to be on her side. "I gotta go Momma. I'm so sorry for putting you through all of this. Momma, please forgive me! I'm so, so sorry for everthing I've done, and kiss my babies for me. Tell them I love and miss them." Then the guard pulled them apart and escorted La Vonne back to her prison cell.

Gloria cries as La Vonne is being lead away, getting out her last words; "La Vonne, I forgive you and I love you! Don't you worry about anything. I'll see to it that you get out of this place soon, I promise."

"Momma, just by being here and knowing that you support and forgive me is more than enough for now. I know that you don't have money to hire a good lawyer, so don't worry about it, I'll figure something else out, you'll see. I love you Momma." La Vonne said just before the door shut closed.

"I love you too baby." Gloria yelled out for her daughter to hear. Then Gloria and her friends hugged each other and cried uncontrollably as they walked toward the outside world.

CHAPTER ELEVEN

Two days have passed since Gloria has seen La Vonne. She's at home with six of the sisters from her church. Three of the ladies, Nancy, Gina and Susan are her best friends. The others; Tina, Samantha and Roxanne, are just a few who seem to invite themselves to anything they can come to be noisy. They're also known as the gossipers of the church. Gloria invited them because she knew they would pass the word around the church that she was in need of everyone's assistance.

Nancy is a sixty-something year old skinny lady with short black and gray hair. She wears coke bottled eyeglasses and is considered as being very nice. Gina is a fifty-something year old medium built lady who is never seen wearing pants. She comes

Momma, Please Forgive Me!

from a family of very strict church goers. Susan is a heavy woman in her late 60's. She seems to always know the answer to every situation. The other ladies between the ages of 45 to 55 and are set in their ways. They are only true friends to each other, because no one else associates with them.

Everyone is sitting in Gloria's living room talking. The gossipers sit together, away from the others and quietly discuss their likes and dislikes of Gloria's small county-styled house. "Um, look at that rocking chair. It looks like she's had it for over twenty years. I bet it's real wood and worth a whole lot of money." Tina whispered. "Well, from what I see, it looks like it's crying out for Sister Gloria to not sit her big butt in it anymore or that real wood will look like plywood soon, because petite and Sister Gloria definitely do not belong in the same sentence. And you'd think that she would have gotten some new glasses by now, those look like she's had them for over twenty years. And her so-called favorite dress, she's been wearing that same dress for at lease ten years, she just keeps adding elastic so it can grow with her big butt." Tina said.

"And look at her hair. It looks like it hasn't been permed in over ten years. I'm sorry to say, but Sister Gloria needs to get it together!" Roxanne said. Then, they quietly laughed.

The other women spoke out loud about the blessings the Lord has done for them. "God is so good to bring all of us together like this." Nancy said. "Yes he is Sister. God is such a good God." Susan responded.

Gloria is happy and in a good mood now that she has seen La Vonne. "Hi everybody." She said as she greeted the ladies and gathered their attention with some tea and butter-cookies.

"Hi Sister Gloria," Gina said. "Hi Sister," Nancy said. "Hi," the rest of the group said as they followed her greeting and helped themselves to the tea and cookies.

"First of all I'd like to thank each and every one of you for coming on such short notice." Gloria said. "Secondly, I need your help." After saying the word help, all of the ladies in the room looked at each other with a dumbfounded expression on their faces. Then Gloria continued; "Now, you all know that La Vonne has been in prison for over two years." The ladies looked at Gloria with serious faces. The gossipers responded; "Yes Sister, we know." Then they looked at each other and frowned.

Gloria continued; "Well, I know my daughter, and she's no criminal. I don't care what anybody says, I tell you, she's no criminal! She's the victim of domestic violence. And I'm sure that some of you know someone who has fallen victim to domestic violence, if it hasn't been you yourself." The very thought of Gloria's words made all the ladies squirm in their chairs.

Then Gloria held up the letter La Vonne sent her. As she held up the letter, everyone looked at the letter, then looked at Gloria and remained quiet. They wanted to know where her comments were leading and what the letter had to do with why they were there. "In the beginning, I had a hard time forgiving La Vonne." Gloria continued. "But after reading this letter, La Vonne proved to me that she did what she felt she had to do in order to protect herself and my precious grandchildren."

The ladies looked at each other and shrugged their shoulders. They were still clueless to Gloria's motives. Gloria looked around the room with a very serious look on her face and continued; "Now, I'm not saying that what La Vonne did was right, but who are we to judge another human being? We've all fallen short of God's good graces. The Lord put it in my heart to finally forgive La Vonne. Now, I'm asking each of you ladies to forgive her as well and help her get out of prison."

The ladies looked at Gloria, then at each other and again moved around uncomfortably in their seats. Shortly after, a few of them spoke; "Oh yes. Sure we can," Gina said. "Sure we can help

Momma, Please Forgive Me!

Sister Gloria, you just tell us what we can do. We all love La Vonne. She is like one of my children." Nancy said. Then Tina explained; "Sister Gloria, we're all Sisters in the Lord." Everyone agreed with the group and together said; "Amen!"

Gloria was very happy with their responses. Her face lit up with joy. "Oh thank God for all of you. The Lord will surely bless each and every one of you." The ladies smiled as Gloria continued; "Well, what I'm trying to do is raise money to pay for a good lawyer that can get La Vonne released from prison. But I can't do it alone, I need your help." Suddenly everyone's expression changed to troubled, concerned looks.

Gloria continued with her plea; "I desperately need your financial help." Suddenly, the ladies tightly clutched their purses. They began looking around the room as if someone were going to snatch their purses out of their hands. "I know that some of you may not be able to help by giving money, but maybe you can help in some other way. For those who can help, I'm sure the Lord will bless you ten fold."

After Gloria paused, the ladies looked at each other with puzzled looks. The gossipers slid down in their chairs, attempting to be unapproachable. The others joined in; "Sure Sister Gloria," Susan said. "I'll see what I can do," Nancy said. "I'll have to pray about it Sister," Gina followed. After her response, the gossipers responded; "Amen," while waving their hands in the air.

Gloria shook her head in acceptance. "I understand all of your concerns. However, before you make any final decisions, go home and pray about it, then, come over in the morning with your answers." They shock their heads in agreement as she continued; "I'm sure God will guide each of you according to His will. I know that I'm asking a lot, but I need you to understand my desire to free my daughter so that she can be home to raise her babies. They desperately need her to be home with them. I pray that you can all understand the sense of my urgency."

The ladies looked at each other, then at Gloria; "Sure, we do Sister Gloria," Nancy said.

"I truly understand Sister, but I can't make any financial decisions without discussing it with Joe first. Ever since we've been married, we've always agreed to share all financial situations with each other before we do anything." Susan said. The others quickly agreed. "Me too Sister."

Then Gina said; "Sister Gloria, you know I love you like my own sister, but this is such a serious situation and I'll have to pray about it and pray for you in this matter; I just don't know." The others again quickly joined in; "Amen."

Gloria knew that she couldn't get everyone to go along with her decision since it had taken two years for her to forgive La Vonne. Therefore, she was pleased that they would at least consider her suggestion. "Ok then, it's settled. Everybody go home and get a good night's rest. Then meet back here in the morning at nine to discuss what God has led each of you to do."

The ladies all agreed, stood up and gathered their belongings. "Sounds good to me Sister," Gina said.

"Me too Sister. I'll see you tomorrow," Susan said as the group agreed. "Amen!"

Gloria hugged each of them as they walked out the door. "Thank you Sisters for coming on such short notice. And thanks for listening. For those who can't see it in your heart to forgive La Vonne, me and God will understand." Then Gloria closed the door as they each went their own way. She felt content, believing that her friends would back her up.

After the house was quiet and empty, Gloria bent down on her knees and prayed to God. "Lord, thank you for my friends. Thank you God for allowing me to see that La Vonne needs me and I need her. Thank you for opening my mind to ways in which

Momma, Please Forgive Me!

I may be able to help her. Lord, please open the hearts and minds of the ladies so that they can see things your way in helping La Vonne. Lord, I believe that your will has already been done. Thank you Lord, Amen." Then Gloria walked to her room, put her bed clothes on and went to sleep, feeling hopeful for tomorrow.

Gloria's best friends; Gina, Susan and Nancy got into Gina's car. Gina was giving them a ride home. "Girl, can you believe the nerve of Sister Gloria?" Susan quickly said after closing the car door. "Now, I love Sister Gloria just like we were blood sisters, but I can't believe she's asking us to help her get that killer out of prison. Once La Vonne gets out, she may kill someone we love. I can't believe that Sister Gloria would ask us to do such a thing at such great risk."

Gina looked at Susan and agreed; "I agree Sister, I can't believe it either. I understand that La Vonne is her daughter and all, but she has only recently forgiven her, herself. So how does she expect for us to forget and forgive so easily. And the nerve of her asking us to give money to get La Vonne out of prison, I don't think so. That's like opening up the door and giving her the key to kill anyone who gets in her way. There's no way in hell, forgive me Lord, that I can do that."

Nancy shook her head in agreement; "Sister's I feel you. But maybe La Vonne has changed. Gloria did say that she did what she did because of her no good husband. She said that he was beating her and those precious little babies. Maybe now that she's been in prison she'll do right by God."

Gina and Susan both looked at Nancy and shook their heads to disagree. "Come on Sister. Do you really think that someone can change after killing someone? Like they say about animals, once they've tasted blood, they'll always want blood. And if someone messes with her or her kids, you can bet your bottom dollar that she'll kill again. I just ain't gonna have no part of being the one to help her get free, especially at the expense of having someone's blood on my hands. No sir." Gina said as she continued to drive.

Nancy and Susan both looked at each other and agreed. "I see your point Sister. I guess when you look at it like that, you're taking a chance of being partially responsible for the death of her next victim. I totally agree." Nancy said. Then Gina dropped them off at their houses and she continued home.

CHAPTER TWELVE

La Vonne is laying in her bed reading a book. There's a dim light shining outside of her cell, which made her reading difficult. Suddenly a visitor appears in the dim shadow, whispering her name through the cell door; "La Vonne, are you still awake?" The strange female voice softly said as La Vonne sat straight up in her bed. The stranger startled La Vonne, causing her to fear the worst. The stranger stood to the side of door, which concealed her identity, along with the dimness of the light.

"Uhhh yeah, I'm still awake. What do you want?" La Vonne asked with fear.

"Can I come in and talk to you?" The stranger said.
La Vonne didn't know what to do. She becomes defensive and panics. She knew that running or hiding weas not an option, so she quickly put her book down and moved toward the rear corner of her bed. Suddenly, the sound of a key moving was heard as the stranger slowly opened her cell door.

"Who is it? And what do you want from me? Why do you want to come in here anyway?" La Vonne said with fear.

"It's me Trina. I just want to talk to you." Immediately La Vonne's fears went away. She knew that Trina was one of the

Momma, Please Forgive Me!

nice guards in the prison. She knew that Trina would not harm her.

"Girl, you scared me. Next time tell me who you are before you sneak up on me like that." Then they laughed.

"I'm sorry. But I thought you could see who I was from the light in the hallway. I didn't mean to scare you, I'm sorry."

La Vonne moved away from the corner and toward the side of her bed to talk. "So, what brings you to my cell this late?" La Vonne said.

"I heard about what happened at your appeal today and I wanted to tell you how sorry I am."

La Vonne was happy for her concern. "Hey, what can I say? I guess I'm going to be in here a little longer than expected." La Vonne was trying to be positive, along with keep a straight face and not cry.

"Everything will be alright. I just wanted to tell you that you don't deserve to be in a place like this. By being a sister and a mother myself, girl, if my husband beat me like yours beat you, I would have killed that bastard with my bear hands!" Trina said while they both quietly laughed.

"Girl, when I heard that you were coming here, I always believed that you got a bad rap. You see, when you killed your man it was during an election term. So, if they would have let you walk, the mayor would not have been re-elected. But that's something you wouldn't know about. Information like that is normally kept under raps, and kept very quiet!" La Vonne shook her head in agreement.

After thinking about the words Trina spoke, La Vonne suddenly became mad and furiously whispered; "You mean to tell me that I was used as an example that allowed the mayor to keep his damn job?"

Trina shook her head in agreement. "It's too bad, but I'm afraid that's what happened darling."

Suddenly all La Vonne could see was red, causing her to become furious. "So, I'm in prison as a fucking example of some damn politics? Ain't that some shit! This is messed up! So what can I do about it?" La Vonne looked at Trina for answers. "Nothing." Trina sadly said.

La Vonne got up and walked around her cell in disbelief. "So it's like that? I can't believe this shit! I just can't believe this."

Then Trina continued; "That's the way I see it. You see, you could never prove that you were sentenced due to politics anyway. Trust me, I've been working for the system far too long to believe differently. La Vonne, I'm telling you this in confidence. Ever since you've been in here you've been really cool and I hate to see you get the short end of the stick." La Vonne was still shaking her head in disbelief as Trina continued.

"Girl, I know that a few bad things have happened to you since you've been here, but there's only so much we guards are able to do to prevent shit like that from happening. There's always a few bad seeds anywhere you go. Unfortunately, we good guards hear about the shit after the damage has already been done. So girl, just hang in there and keep fighting. Don't let the judge's decision get you down. Well, I gotta go now. I also wanted to tell you that if there's anything I can do to help, let me know."
La Vonne stood up and hugged Trina for her concern and support. "Thanks, I'll do that."

Then Trina walked toward the door and walked out. "Like I said, let me know if there's anything I can do for you, and I mean anything! I also believe that you should be at home raising your own kids, not your mother raising them for you. Like I said earlier, I may work for the system, but I don't believe that everything they say is right." Trina locked the cell door. "So hang in there."

La Vonne was happy that someone felt the same way she did, giving her hope to continue her fight for freedom. "Thanks, I really appreciate the support. It's people like you who help make a bad situation not so bad. Thanks again." La Vonne said as Trina smiled.

"No problem. Now, get some sleep." Then Trina walked away and went back to work. La Vonne walked toward her bed, laid down, rolled over and fell fast a sleep.

CHAPTER THIRTEEN

It's early morning and the sun has recently risen. Due to the dark curtains, preventing the sun from shining into Gloria's bedroom, she is not awake. All of a sudden she's awakened by the ringing of the telephone. The loud sound of the ringer startled her, causing her to jump and sit straight up in her bed. She quickly grabbed the phone; "Hello?" she said in a short and unpleasant tone.

Nancy was amazed by Gloria's unpleasant tone; "Sister Gloria, is that you?"

Gloria cleared her throat and rephrased her tone; "Yes, it's me. Who is this?"

Nancy laughed as she realized she had awakened Gloria. "This is Nancy. Did I wake you?"

"Don't worry about it, I need to get up anyway. Sorry for sounding so short," Gloria pleasantly said.

"I'm sorry I woke you Sister."

"No problem. What can I do for you this morning?"

"Well, I talked things over with Frank and I won't be able to help you. He doesn't want me to get involved with any legal stuff like that. He thinks something bad might happen to our family if I get involved. So, I'm sorry I can't help," Nancy nervously awaited Gloria's response.

Gloria was disappointed to hear her words. She and Nancy

had been friends for years. Gloria felt that Nancy would help her no matter what the situation involved, however, she didn't want Nancy to feel obligated. "I understand."

Nancy could tell by Gloria's tone that she was disappointed. She also knew she didn't want to get involved, no matter what her husband had to say. "Bye Sister Gloria and good luck. I'll pray for you and La Vonne."

"Thank you." Gloria said as she quickly hung up the telephone, not allowing Nancy to give her another excuse of pity.

Gloria got out of bed to get dressed. Suddenly the telephone rang again; "Hello," she said.

"Hi Sister Gloria. This is Sister Gina," Gloria paused, waiting to hear what she had to say.

"Sister, I won't be able to come by this morning." Gloria was confused, but remained quiet, allowing her to continue. "I forgot that I had some important business to handle today, and no one else can take care of it, but me. Susan also told me to tell you that she wouldn't be able to make it over this morning either. She said she would call you later and explain. So, tell the ladies that we said 'hi' and that we wish all of you luck today. Let us know how things work out for La Vonne. We'll keep her in our prayers."

Gloria was disappointed by her so-called besst friends. However, she tried to keep her true feelings to herself. "Thank you for calling," she said in a somber tone. "I understand, bye."

"Bye Sister Gloria. I'll check on you later."

Gloria again did not want to hear anything else from her so-called friend. "Thank you, but we'll manage just fine, good bye." Then Gloria hung up the telephone.

From the sounds of Gloria's tone, Gina knew she had hurt her feelings. Nevertheless, she felt that she did what she had to do, feeling no regrets.

After Gloria hung up the telephone she dropped down onto

Momma, Please Forgive Me!

her knees and prayed; "Oh Lord God, please Lord, help my friends see the light. Help them find forgiveness in their hearts. Lord, I can't blame them for not wanting to be involved, because it took me two years to open my heart to my own daughters mistakes. Forgiveness is a lot to ask of someone, as it was to even ask of myself. What was I thinking? Lord, it's now up to you to make a way. I can only do what you allow me to do and nothing more. Lord, you know that La Vonne shouldn't be locked away in that filthy place this long. It's up to you as to what will happen with her fate now. I'm trusting in you to make a way for La Vonne. Help me to help her come home. Thank you Lord, Amen." Then Gloria went to get dressed.

After she was dressed, Gloria fixed coffee, just in case someone showed up for the scheduled meeting. To her surprise, the doorbell rang. Gloria walked toward the long mirror hanging on the wall and looked at herself. She wanted to be assured that she was presentable for the unknown visitor. She quickly walked toward the door and opened it. Once opened, a big smile appeared on her face as the ladies who were considered the gossipers proudly stood at her door. "Surprise!" they all said with big smiles on their faces. Gloria opened the door and they walked inside and sat down, making themselves at home.

At that very moment Gloria was faced with reality. Their arrival reminded her about the valuable lesson of not judging others. This very lesson was one Pastor Ron preached regularly, although, Gloria had not taken heed to it very well, until now. Gloria knew that she had always been there for her so-called best friends. However, she didn't understand why they couldn't be there during her time of need? She finally realized that Nancy, Susan and Gina weren't the true friends she believed they were, otherwise they would have been there for her, no matter what the situation involved.

After the ladies made themselves at home, Gloria looked to God, raised her hands up high, smiled and thought; "Thank you Jesus. Thank you! I knew you'd come through for me." Then she closed the door feeling good! She offered her new friends coffee while they pulled chairs out of the kitchen to sit in a circle. Then, they put their heads together to come up with a plan that would help La Vonne become free.

CHAPTER FOURTEEN

It's mid-afternoon. La Vonne has been summoned to come to the visitors room to meet with her waiting visitor. She's curious and happy as to who's waiting for her, knowing it wouldn't be Ron since she fired him. She assumes it's Pastor George. His visits always cheer her up and she looks forward to them.

As she walks into the room, her face lights up; "Hi Momma," she says with excitement. "What are you all doing here?" She hugs Gloria while noticing the ladies who are with her. While hugging La Vonne as tight as she could, Gloria is so excited she blares out; "We're gonna help you get out of this filthy place, that's what we're doing here." she boastfully said.

La Vonne is so excited to see and hug her mom, yet puzzled; "How Momma? How are you guys going to help me? You don't have the kind of money it takes to pay for a good lawyer. Lets face it, a public defense lawyer is not going to get me out of here. I need someone as good as Johnnie Cochran if I'm ever going to get out of here."

Then everybody laughed. "Well, if I could afford Mr. Cochran, believe me baby, you'd have Mr. Cochran," Gloria said as they continued laughing.

Gloria's tone immediately changed, becoming very

serious; "Look here La Vonne, what's the one thing I've always taught you baby?"

La Vonne looked at her mother; "That if we pray, believe and ask for forgiveness, God will do the rest." Gloria hugged her and smiled; "That's my girl." Suddenly everybody in the room smiled.

"Momma, I have asked God for forgiveness and I do believe. But so far that plan hasn't worked for me." La Vonne's tone was very somber. "I'm still locked up. So now what do we do?"

Gloria took La Vonne's chin in her hand and looked her straight in the eyes; "Honey, we'll get you out of here. You just leave everything up to me and these wonderful ladies. We're all going to work together to get you the best lawyer money can buy."

Suddenly La Vonne's somber tone changed to excitement; "I believe you. So, what plan do you have in mind?" Gloria looked at the ladies, then she looked at La Vonne; "If it takes hiring Johnnie Cochran to get you out of this dump, then some how Johnnie is who we'll hire! Then, we're all going to celebrate."

La Vonne smiled and hugged her mom; "I love you Momma. I knew one day you'd forgive me. Pastor George said you would."

Gloria looked at La Vonne with a puzzled expression on her face; "You've talked to Pastor George?"

"He comes to see me every month. He's one of the reasons I've remained so strong all these years. By knowing that one day I'll be free and back with my children is the other reason I've been so strong. Pastor George always tells me to keep praying and one day you would forgive me. I told him not to tell you that he was coming. I wanted you to forgive me on your own. I didn't want you to forgive me because of his, or anyone else's influence."

After hearing La Vonne, Gloria began to cry; "Baby, I'm

sorry it took me so long to come around. I didn't know what you and those precious babies had been through all those years. I didn't know that you were living in such horror. I guess I was too proud to admit that my daughter could do such a thing. My pride got in the way of understanding your pain and giving you my forgiveness. But all that's in the past now. God has taught me how to be a better person and how to forgive. He showed me that things don't always happen the way they should. He reminded me that if he could forgive us of our sins, we should be able to forgive others of theirs. So, now I'm here to help you. All of us will work hard to get you out of here. Isn't that right ladies?" Gloria looked at the ladies for their support.

    The ladies looked at Gloria, and then at La Vonne, smiled and agreed; "Amen!" Then they hugged Gloria and La Vonne and started singing 'Glory Hallelujah' while happily dancing in the small room while praising God in the spirit.

    Later that afternoon Gloria went to see Pastor George. Their church has a very large congregation, however, the size of the congregation does not prevent him from knowing all of his members. In fact, he makes it a point to learn everyone's name as they join the church family.

    Gloria walks to the door of Pastor George's office. His secretary is away from her desk as she enters. Gloria walks toward the door of the Pastor's office and knocks on the cracked door; "Pastor, are you here?" she says as she peaks into the door that opens wide. Pastor George looks her way and turns toward the voice. "Hi Pastor. Can I come in? I didn't see your secretary out there. I hope I'm not intruding."

    Pastor George stands up from his chair, walks toward Gloria and extends his arms to give Gloria a friendly hug; "Hi Sister Gloria. Come on in and have a seat." Gloria pulls out a chair and sits down. "What can I do for you?" he says as she sits in the big

Momma, Please Forgive Me!

leather chair.

"Pastor, I just returned from a long and overdue visit with La Vonne," she says with a little pride and embarrassment in her voice. "That's good to hear Sister, go on," he urged. "Pastor, La Vonne told me that you've been visiting her. She also said that your visits have encouraged her to stay strong. I just wanted to thank you." Then she put her head down in shame and cried.

Pastor George smiled at Gloria's response; "Sister Gloria, you know better than that." She immediately looked up, wiped her tears and smiled as he continued; "After all the years I've known you and La Vonne, you don't need to thank me for anything. We're family here. We should always be there to help our sisters and brothers, no matter what the situation involves, no one is sinless. All of us have fallen short of God's good grace at some point or another. God is the only one who should judge others, not us. La Vonne just took a wrong turn. Now she needs our guidance to get back on the right track. I'm glad to know that my words have helped her through this rough time."

Gloria felt good hearing his words; "Pastor, I need your help." He was interested in what she had to say. "Anything Sister, just name it." Gloria proceeded; "La Vonne fired her attorney and now she needs a new one. But my funds are very low. She desperately needs our help to get out of there. Pastor, you know she doesn't belong in there. She belongs at home with her children. Is there anyway you can help?" Gloria's solemn expression made Pastor George feel sorry. He knew he needed to come up with a solution that would work.

"I wondered how her lawyer was working out. She never wanted to talk about him when I came to see her. She always told me that things were working out and that he was working hard on her case. Sister, I'll tell you what I'm gonna do for Sister La Vonne. On Sunday, we'll take a special collection in her honor.

With the money we receive, we should be able to get a good lawyer to at least start on her case. Then, we'll pray for the additional money that would pay the lawyers bill in full. Sister, just remember that God can do all!" Then he stood up, held her hands in his and prayed as Gloria cried.

"Excuse me for crying Pastor, but I just can't help feeling bad for La Vonne. Maybe if I would have helped her sooner, she would've been home long before now." He gave her a tissue and walked around the table to console her.

"Sister Gloria, stop that right now! I don't ever want to hear you blame yourself. You did what you thought you had to do. I believe your motives were done to protect your precious grandchildren. You must not forget that you've given them all the love and support they've needed in order to get on with their lives during the absence of their parents. You just needed time to come around in order to focus on La Vonne. I agree that La Vonne made a bad decision, but that's all in the past, and the idea of you not wanting to forgive her is also all in the past. Now, we must concentrate on making things right for the future. So, put your time and effort into helping her, not into faulting yourself for what you thought you should have done. Leave the past in the past! Do you hear me?" Gloria looked at him through her tears and smiled. He smiled with her.

"Thank you Pastor. Thank you so very much. This entire ordeal has been so hard on me. I have to believe that everything will be alright," Gloria now felt more confident as she spoke to Pastor George.

"That's what I want to hear. So, go out and find La Vonne the best lawyer money can buy. Then let God do the rest!" he said as he walked her toward the door.

"I will Pastor. Thank you again for everything." Then she slowly walked out of the Pastor's office. His words encouraged

Momma, Please Forgive Me!

her faith, allowing her to face her new mission of freeing her daughter and bringing her home to be with her children.

Shortly after leaving Pastor George's office, Gloria arrives home. As she walks through the door the telephone rings. She runs to answer it; "Hello," she says. "Hello, Sister Gloria. This is Pastor George. How are you doing?" Gloria smiles, but is surprised by his sudden call. "I'm feeling fine Pastor, thanks for asking. Did I leave something in your office?"

"No, you didn't. I just wanted to pass on some good news," he says. Gloria is so excited. She reacts like a child; "What good news? What is it Pastor, tell me!"

He laughs; "Calm down Sister, calm down. I just got off the phone with an old member of the church who moved out of the area. He's a lawyer. Now, from what I remember he's a very good lawyer. In fact, some have compared his style to that of the infamous, Mr. Johnnie Cochran. Anyway Sister, he's agreed to take on La Vonne's case."

Gloria screams; "Oh my God! Oh my God! Thank you Pastor, thank you very much!"

Pastor George again laughs at her reaction and continues; "Sister Gloria let me finish."

Gloria was so excited that she had to make herself settle down; "Ok go ahead, I'm listening."

He continued; "Anyway, he has not only agreed to take La Vonne's case, but he's also agreed to write off all of his attorney fees. So, how's that for God's intervention?"

Gloria again couldn't remain calm; "Oh my God! Oh my God! I don't believe what I'm hearing. I just don't believe it!" Pastor George was getting a kick out of her enthusiasm; "Well, believe it Sister, just believe it. But I have to go now. I'll put my secretary on the line and she'll give you all the information you need on Jay. Then you can set up an appointment to go and see him. So take care and I'll put her on." Gloria was so excited that she was shaking. She didn't know what to do. "Ok, thank you Pastor. Thank you so very much!"

"You're welcome." He happily responded. Then he put his secretary on the phone who gives Gloria the details.

CHAPTER FIFTEEN

The next day Gloria proudly walked to the front door of Bethel "Jay" Mitchell, Attorney at Law. She is nervous, but confident. She's dressed to kill in a navy blue suit with a white buttoned silk blouse, high heel shoes and a navy blue purse to match. She's also wearing a fashionable large round navy blue hat that has a white long feather along the side. She walks into the office and goes toward the desk of his secretary. After getting her attention, Gloria introduces herself; "Hello, my name is Gloria Johnson. I have an appointment with Mr. Mitchell."

The secretary looks at Gloria and smiles; "Have a seat Miss Johnson. I'll tell Mr. Mitchell you've arrived, he's expecting you."

"Thank you." Gloria said with pride as she walks toward the plush black leather seats in the waiting area. Gloria is very impressed with the specialized treatment she's receiving. She sits down in one of the large plush seats and admires the beautiful African-American artwork on the walls. One of the pictures she recognizes is a painting by Synthia St. James. Gloria thinks: "I've seen that picture before. I know I've seen that picture before, but where? Oh yeah, that's the same picture I have at home in my African-American stamp collection. The Kwanzaa stamp, but a whole lot bigger!" She doesn't recognize the other paintings. The entire office is decorated in a very upscale fashion. Soft urban music is playing throughout the intercom system.

Momma, Please Forgive Me!

Just as Gloria's getting comfortable, the secretary walks up to her; "Excuse me Miss Johnson. Mr. Mitchell will see you now. Come this way please."

"Thank you," Gloria says as the secretary personally escorts her down the hallway that leads to Jay's office. After reaching his office, the secretary opens the door for Gloria to walk in. Once inside, Jay, a very attractive African-American man who is handsomely dressed, stands to greet Gloria.

At the first glance, Gloria smiles, blushing at his attractive looks. However, she regains her professional composer, remembering why she came. She also realizes that Jay is young enough to be her son.

He smiles and extends his hand for her to shake; "Welcome Miss Johnson. I'm glad you could make it. I've been expecting you."

Gloria's face beamed with joy; "Hello Mr. Mitchell. Thank you for seeing me at such short notice."

Then Jay directed her to sit in a plush leather chair that faced his desk. "Have a seat," he said as she sat down. Then he continued; "Before we begin, if we're going to be working closely together you must call me Jay. Mr. Mitchell is much too formal." Gloria smiled; "Ok Jay."

When he smiled back he displayed all of his beautiful pearly white teeth and continued; "Pastor George has already told me about your daughter's case. In fact, I'm a little familiar with her case already. I remember reading her story in the newspaper a few years ago. I always believed the young lady in the story got the short end of the stick. In fact, if it wasn't an election year she may have never went to prison. Unfortunately, that's one of the disadvantages when it comes to politics. However, after time passed, I never heard anything else about the case. I assumed things had worked out for her."

Gloria shook her head to disagree with his statement. "Unfortunately, things never did work out for her. That's why we desperately need your help. Pastor George spoke highly of your talents as a lawyer. He said that if anybody could free her from prison, you would be the one to do it. So now, I'm counting on you. Because frankly, you're all we have. You're our last and only hope of seeing her released from that filthy place they call a prison. After visiting her the other day and seeing it for myself, I wouldn't let my dogs live there, let alone a human being."

Jay could see the hurt and pain in Gloria's eyes. He knew that she had come to the right lawyer; "Thank you and thank Pastor George for me. Your kind words mean a lot because I've always admired Pastor George. We lost contact with each other after I moved. My practice became so busy that it took me to another area. Now, I'm too far away to commute every Sunday for church services. However, I've found a church home closer to where I live. I only visit Pastor George's church when I can."

"Well, as long as you stay strong in the Lord it doesn't matter which church you go to."

Jay smiled and continued; "When Pastor George called me last night I was ready and willing to help in anyway I could."
"The Lord will bless you."

Jay smiled; "Thank you. He already has, in more ways than you can imagine. Now, lets get to work and get La Vonne out of that place." Together, they worked on a plan toward freeing La Vonne.

****

Later that night Gloria and the kids are at home sleep. After a very successful day with Jay, Gloria is finally able to sleep peacefully since La Vonne's arrest two years ago. As she dreamt peaceful thoughts, she is suddenly awakened by loud screams and yells; "Daddy, stop hitting mommy. You're hurting her. Please stop! Please daddy, stop! Daddy!" She quickly jumps out of bed and runs toward Jr.'s room. He's having another nightmare about the fateful fight between his mother and father.

As Gloria reaches his room, she goes over to his bed and shakes him to wake him up; "Jr., wake up baby. Wake up. It's alright. Grandma's here with you now. It's alright baby, stop crying. Grandma's here!" He immediately wakes up and begins crying. He grabs Gloria and holds her as tight as he can.

In an effort to console him, Gloria rocks him back and forth in her arms; "Calm down baby, Grandma's right here. Nothing bad is going to happen to you. Calm down. It's alright." Finally, Gloria's soothing words calm him down, allowing him to fall fast asleep in her arms. Gloria lays him down on his bed, covers him up and walks back to her room and prays; "Dear Lord God, please help that precious little child. Lord, help him get over that dreadful night. Help him get pass the fear of watching his mother kill his father. Lord God he needs your help to ease his pain. Help him understand that everything will soon be alright. Amen." Then she gets into her bed, rolls over and quickly falls fast asleep.

CHAPTER SIXTEEN

It's the next day, after Gloria has spoken with Jay. La Vonne has been summoned to the prison meeting room. To her surprise she finds Gloria standing there with opened arms. Standing next to Gloria is Jay, who is dressed to a tee, looking important and standing tall. He is an unfamiliar face to La Vonne, but a welcomed sight for her to admire; "Hi Momma," she said as she smiles. While hugging her mom, La Vonne stares over Gloria's shoulder and admires Jay from the corner of her eye.

Gloria is very excited. She knows that her news will definitely brighten La Vonne's day. "Hi baby," Gloria says as she lets go of La Vonne and looks at Jay. "Baby, I'd like you to meet Mr. Bethel Jay Mitchell."

Jay extends his hand for La Vonne to shake. La Vonne blushes and happily returns the gesture. "Hello Miss Brown," Jay says with a low and inviting baritone sound to his voice.

Due to his sexy sounding voice, La Vonne is blushing like a school girl. Hearing Jay's voice has made her the happiest she's been since she's arrived in prison. "Ms. Brown?" Jay says as La Vonne cuts him off; "Oh no Mr. Mitchell, please call me La Vonne."

By reacting his normal and polite self, he again shows his famous smile and responds; "Ok La Vonne, call me Jay. How are you doing?"

Suddenly La Vonne blushes even more, hoping that his smile was something special for only her. She could not control her gestures, nor did she care to do so. Watching her smile was a welcome sight to Gloria. "I'm fine now that you're here," La Vonne responds. Then she looks at Gloria with a puzzled look in her eye; "So Momma, what are you doing here today? Is something going on that I missed?" La Vonne was hoping that the something that was going on had something to do with Jay being there.

Gloria was getting a kick in watching La Vonne's expressions and started telling her the good news; "La Vonne, Jay is your new lawyer."

Suddenly La Vonne's mouth opened wide, leaving her speechless. She was confused, yet very happy and excited to hear what Gloria had just announced. After listening to her words, she stood in total shock, looking lifeless. She didn't know anything else to do but stand in silence. However, after hearing her

Momma, Please Forgive Me!

mother's joyous words, she was sure that there was a God in heaven looking over her.

Eventually she regained from her trance, grabbed Gloria's hand, walked to a corner and whispered; "My new lawyer? Did you say that he is my new lawyer?" Gloria shook her head in agreement and smiled as La Vonne continued; "Momma, how did you pull that off and so quick? You don't have that kind of money to pay for a fancy and good-looking lawyer like Jay." La Vonne's eyes stayed focused on Jay, as he looked through his briefcase.

"Baby, Pastor George referred Jay to us. They have already worked out the details amongst themselves. So don't you worry about anything. Jay is here to help!" Gloria said with pride and confidence.

La Vonne was still blown away by the wonderful news. The way Jay looked, she didn't care if he was a minister who only came to say a prayer for her. The only thing she cared about was that he would continue to come back.

"La Vonne, your mother's right. Don't worry about the money. Everything has been worked out. All you need to worry about is me getting you released from prison." Jay said with confidence.

The words he spoke were music to La Vonne's ears. She began to daydream pleasant thought of him and her together as a couple throughout his conversation. She didn't care what else he had to say, just as long as he kept saying that he would be coming back to see her.

"La Vonne," he said as she watched his every move. "I want to hear your side of what happened on the night you killed your husband. I've already heard everyone else's point of view, now I want to hear yours. Your point of view is what I'll build my case around. So don't leave out any details whatsoever!"

After Jay's instructions, all three of them sat down at the

table to develop a strategy that would set La Vonne free.

****

It's late in the afternoon. Gloria has just come home from her meeting with Jay and La Vonne. She's in a very good mood. As soon as she steps into the door she sees her grandchildren; "Hi babies! How are you doing?" They run toward her and hug onto her waist.

"Hi Grandma. Where have you been all day long?" Jr. said. Before Gloria could answer, Stacy joined in; "Yeah Grandma. Where have you been? I was looking for you."

Gloria smiles and responds; "I had some business to take care of, that's all."

Stacy looks up at her with a puzzled look on her face; "What kind of business Grandma?"

Then Jr. responds; "Grown folks business silly." Together, everyone laughs, including Rae, who was babysitting the kids. Gloria looks at Stacy and reaffirms Jr.'s comment; "That's right, grown folks business, that's what I was doing."

Stacy has no idea what they're all laughing at, nor does she know what grown folks business is. "Grandma, what's grown folks business?" she said in a very serious tone.

Gloria sits down in her favorite rocking chair, pulls off her shoes, sits Stacy on her lap and explains. She didn't want to tell the children exactly where she was because she didn't want their expectations to be overwhelmed. "Well child, grown folks business is business that only adults like myself and Rae can take care of. It's the kind of business that children don't know anything about. Do you understand now?" Then Gloria looked at Stacy for a response.

Stacy threw her arms up in the air and responded; "I guess I understand Grandma."

With Stacy only being eight years old and Jr. ten, Gloria felt that that was all the explaining she needed to do for now.

Momma, Please Forgive Me!

Therefore she changed the subject; "So, how are my two little angels doing today? Did you have fun with Rae while I was gone?" Gloria looked at Rae and smiled.

Stacy became all excited as she answered; "Yeah! We had a lot of fun playing hide and seek. Rae played with us too."

Jr. also became excited and decided to add in his two cents; "But I won Grandma. I found them every time they hid. They couldn't hide from me." he smiled, feeling proud.

Stacy decided to defend her honor; "No you didn't! I found you one time."

"One time, big deal. I still won! Because I found you and Rae a hundred times." he again defended himself.

However, Stacy was determined to get the last word in; "No you didn't!"

Jr. knew he was getting her upset, so he continued; "Yes I did! Now, what you gonna do about it? Ha, ha ha!" he teased.

Then she stuck out her tongue in his direction and made an ugly face. After making the face, Jr. chased Stacy around the room. "Grandma, tell her to stop licking her tongue at me, or I'm going to hit her!"

Gloria's happy and calm tone suddenly changed to that of authority. She sat up in her chair, chapped her hands together loud and roared; "Both of you better stop running around this house right now! And there will be no hitting anybody in this house, unless it's me who's doing the hitting! And I'll be hitting on both of your butts if you don't stop right now! You know better than that, now don't you? Or do I need to remind you?"

They immediately stopped in their tracks and answered in fear; "No Grandma, we remember!"

Rae looked the other way, trying to not display her laughter to their frightened answer. The children knew that their grandmother meant business. They also knew to not cross her.

"Now that you two have settled down, let me tell you about my day. It was pretty good." Gloria said, while peaking everyone's interest.

"What kind of fun did you have Grandma?" Jr. said with an interested look on his face.

"Well, I was going to keep it a surprise. But I can't hold it from you any longer. I'm too excited." With these words Gloria really had everyone's attention. Her face was glowing as she spoke, causing their interest to peak higher.

"What is it Grandma? Is it the grown folks business you told us about before?" Stacy said. Everyone laughed at her response.

"Yes baby, it is." Then she explained; "But this grown folks business is something you can understand. In fact, this grown folks business will make both of you very happy."

The kids started jumping up and down, waiting to hear the good news. "What is it? What is it Grandma?" Jr. said in a very excited and impatient tone.

"Calm down, I'll tell you everything. But you have to calm down first." Gloria said, then continued her announcement. "But, before I tell you the news, I want both of you to sit down on my lap."

Both of the kids ran to her lap and quickly sat down. Their faces had expressions of joy and excitement. Their expressions were those of how they would look after walking into a large room filled with Christmas gifts, bought especially for them. "Ok, are you ready for my news?" Gloria said with excitement.

"We're ready! We're ready!" everyone said. Even Rae joined in on the excitement. "I'm ready too."

"Well, I saw your mom today." Jr. and Stacy looked at each other, smiled and waited for more.

"Yeah! Yeah! When is she coming home Grandma?" they said full of excitement.

Momma, Please Forgive Me!

"Slow down, slow down!" Gloria said and continued: "It may take a little while to get her out of prison, but I found a new lawyer that will help her come home to us." Stacy looked confused. "Grandma, what's a lawyer?" she said with innocence in her voice. Gloria had protected her grandchildren from anything that dealt with law or their mother, causing them to be confused and unaware.

"Silly, a lawyer is a?" Jr. said with confidence when suddenly his confident attitude changed; "Yeah Grandma! Exactly what is a lawyer?"

Everyone laughed as Gloria proceeded; "Child, you're something else. Now sit still and let me explain," she said while shaking her head, smiling. "A lawyer is a person who tries to help people when they're in trouble, like your mom."

Jr. looked at Gloria, still puzzled. "Grandma, is this lawyer going to help our mommy come home?"
She smiled; "That's exactly what he's going to do."

After Gloria's explanation, Jr. and Stacy became so excited they jumped out of her lap. They started jumping up and down, while dancing throughout the entire room. "YEAH!!!! Mommy's coming home! YEAH!!!" they both yelled. Rae watches and enjoys the excitement of the kids, knowing how much the good news means to them.

As Gloria watches their excitement, it assures her that she did the right thing by telling them she saw their mother. This exciting news also assures the kids, by giving them the added faith that their prayers would one day be answered. "Ok, that's enough dancing," Gloria tells them. "It's getting late and you two need to go to school in the morning. So dance yourselves into your bedroom so you can get some sleep."

"Ok Grandma. But when can we see her? When?" an excited Jr. said.

Stacy joined in; "Yeah, can we? Can we Grandma? I miss

her so much!"

Jr. added; "Yeah, I miss her too. Can we go tomorrow, after school?"

Stacy's eyes lit up; "Yeah, can we? Can we Grandma?" she said while jumping up and down in front of Gloria. Rae laughed at their reactions while Gloria smiled and shook her head.

"Slow down you two. I'll have to talk to her lawyer and see if kids can visit. You see, a prison is not a nice place for anyone to be. It's sure not a nice place for innocent children like you two to ever be. But since we're talking about visiting your mom, who you miss very much, we'll see if an exception can be made. So, until her lawyer says it's alright, don't keep asking me. Do you hear me?" Gloria said with a firm tone. Suddenly the children's expressions turned sad, but they understood. "Ok Grandma, we won't ask," they said with their heads hanging down low.

Gloria knew they were upset with her answer, but she also knew she had to keep their best interest in mind until La Vonne was able to come home. "Now, go to bed. It's way past your bedtime and make it quick!" she said with her usual firm voice of authority, while smiling. Through her warning, the kids noticed her smile and joined her, also giving her a big hug before they left the room.

"Goodnight Grandma. I love you!" Jr. said as Stacy added; "I love you too Grandma, goodnight!"

Gloria hugged them as tight as she could, which was one of her specialities they learned to enjoy. "Goodnight my little angels. I love you too." Then she let them go as they ran to their bedroom.

After the kids went to their room, Rae gathered her belongings to go home. "Well, I'm gonna go now, unless you need me to stay longer."

Gloria smiled; "No thank you Rae. Thanks for watching the kids for me. I sure appreciate your help."

Momma, Please Forgive Me!

Rae smiled; "Any time Gloria. If you need me again just call, I'm right next door. I know you need to handle your business," she said as she walked out the door.

"I sure do. Thanks again. Bye." Gloria said as she closed the door. Then she walked to her bedroom and changed her clothes so that she could prepare for another day.

CHAPTER SEVENTEEN

It's late at night and La Vonne is in her prison cell laying on the bed. All of the main lights in the prison are turned off, making the area very dim and hard to see anything. She's thinking about her day, which put her thoughts on cloud nine. Her thoughts gave her a more realistic hope of becoming free. "Momma always said that if I just prayed and believed in my prayers, God would see me through the bad times."

While La Vonne thought about her day, someone came to her cell door and whispered; "Hey La Vonne, are you still awake?" Due to the dimness of the light, La Vonne's good thoughts turned to those of being frightened because she did not know who was at the door. She slowly and cautiously rolled over and responded; "Yeah, why?"

The mystery voice continued; "It's me, Trina. How's things going?"

After hearing that the mystery voice was Trina, La Vonne's frightened thoughts disappeared as she got out of her bed to go toward the door. "Hi Trina. Things are actually going very well! My mother got me a new lawyer, and girl, the man is fine! With all capitals 'FINE!'" Then they both laughed as La Vonne continued; "Anyway, he said that he would get me out of this place. I sure hope it's soon."

"Girl I know what you mean." Trina said. "It'll be soon, don't you worry. Personally, I think that if you have someone find some dirt on that bastard of a husband you had, you would be able to get out with no problem!" La Vonne was pleasantly interested in Trina's explanation because she had never thought about doing that, nor had her old lawyer ever suggested such an idea. "Some dirt? What kind of dirt are you talking about? Do you know some?" La Vonne said with curiosity.

"No, I personally don't know anything about him. But I'm sure that that bastard wasn't a saint either. I would bet my bottom dollar that he had some kind of dirty skeleton left in his closet before you killed his black ass. Wasn't there something he did that he didn't want anybody else to know about?"

La Vonne had an unusual look on her face while Trina continued; "Think girl. There's got to be something that he did that would make your case stronger. You were married to him, think hard! By finding out at least one of his skeletons could be the only way to get you out of this place. There was a girl locked up in here awhile ago who shouldn't have been in here and that's what she did to get out. She found some dirt on her ex, which proved that she was in fear of her life. The judge released her due to the grounds of her being in danger. So think harder! It may be your only chance of getting out of here."

La Vonne had a puzzled look in her eye while listening to Trina. "Hmm, let me think about that, because a saint was the farthest thing related to Jonathan."

Trina smiled; "See, keep thinking. I'm sure you can come up with something. But it has to be good in order for a judge to buy it and grant you another appeal. Because getting an appeal is not easy. So it has to be something good!"

La Vonne continued to think, while Trina continued to jog her memory. "Girl, the way I see it, as much as your man did drugs

Momma, Please Forgive Me!

and partied like an animal, he had to have left at least one bad skeleton behind. These skeletons will help prove that he's a dirty and mean motha' fucka'. Think girl, think hard if you want to get out of here. And if that lawyer is as fine as you say he is, then your ass better be thinking in double time so you can get out of here and get with him, if you know what I mean?" Then they laughed.

"You're right. He had to have done something that would prove that we were in danger and that he was a dirty son-of-a-bitch before I killed his black ass. Thanks Trina, let me think about everything you said. You gave me something very valuable to think about." La Vonne now had added confidence.

Trina smiled; "That's my girl. Now, go do your homework and get out of this crazy place. You don't belong in here. This place is for crazy fools and you ain't one of em'."

"Thanks girl." La Vonne's confidence was growing stronger than ever. However, her confidence suddenly fell short; "Hey, do you really think I'd have a chance in hell to get a date with my fine lawyer when I get out? Do you think he would want to be with an ex-prisoner? Because I did actually kill someone? He might be afraid that I'll kill him if her messes up."

Trina looked at La Vonne who had a body most women would die for, but tried hard to hide it from the other inmates by wearing oversized prison clothes. Trina also knew that La Vonne had a very nice personally which she knew could attract any red-blooded man in need; "I'll put it like this girlfriend, he's a man and he has needs just like any other man. Besides, after all the time you've spent in this place, I'm sure that satisfying the needs of a good man would be the least of your worries, if you know what I mean. Hell, I can bet that when you do get a man, you'll whip some good lovin' on him so good, that his head will be spinning!" They laughed out loud, then covered their mouths to keep their laughter to themselves.

"You got that right!" La Vonne agreed as they gave each other a high five through the cell bars.

"Well girl, I gotta go back to work." Trina said.

"I understand."

Trina continued; "What can I say other than a girls got to make a living doing something, even if it's dealing with all these hard heads around here."

"Well, thanks again." La Vonne said as she walked toward her bed.

"No problem. I hope everything works out for you. See ya later, gotta get back to my beat now. Hopefully nobody has broken out while I've been talking to you, or I'll some explaining as to why I'm just now finding out." Trina said and laughed as she walked away, checking into the rooms of the other prisoners, making sure everyone was accounted for.

La Vonne laid down on her bed and thought about their conversation. "Hmm, I wonder if a man like Jay really would be interested in me. I guess it's something to think about, especially if he's not married. But right now, I need to concentrate on ways that will get me out of here, ways that will shed a new light on Jonathan. Because it doesn't make any since in making plans for Jay if I'm still locked up in here. With his good looks and brains, I'm sure a jail bird is the last thing he needs."

Then La Vonne closes her eyes and drifts off to sleep. As her pleasant thoughts continue, she suddenly begins to hear noises throughout the prison. These noises are those of female prisoners satisfying each others sexual needs. The noises upset her, causing her to attempt to block them out of her mind by covering her ears with her pillow. These are noises that she has grown accustomed to hearing and falls asleep with her pillow over her head. During her sleep, La Vonne begins to dream. Her dream causes her to become agitated, causing her to toss and turn.

"Jonathan, please don't take another drink. Please, don't keep doing this to our family. Please stop!" La Vonne quietly says while she sleeps. Suddenly, she hears the voice of Jonathan responding; "Bitch, don't tell me what to do in my own damn house! I told you to get away from me with that shit. You and those damn kids get the hell away from me right now, or else!"

Suddenly, she wakes up, looking around the room in a cold sweat. She realizes that she was dreaming about the many beatings Jonathan gave her while her kids watched in horror, and while she tried to keep her family together. She then rolled over and went back to sleep, knowing that even though she was locked away in prison, she was safe from his beatings.

CHAPTER EIGHTEEN

It's early in the morning at Gloria's house. Gloria is awake and in a good mood. She has spoken to Jay. She has good news for her grandchildren who are still asleep. She can't wait for them to wait up so she wakes them; "Wake up kids! Wake up!" Gloria says with excitement in her voice as she continues; "You guys aren't going to school today, instead, we're going to see your mom!" After hearing Gloria's words, the kids begin to wake up and wipe their eyes. They're still unsure of what they heard. "Wake up! I said we're going to see your mom today!"

Finally, they realize what she has said and start jumping on their beds with excitement. "Grandma, did you say that we're going to see our mom today?" Stacy said with an excited, but confused look on her face.

Jr. too looked at Gloria with uncertainty; "Yeah Grandma, is that what you said?"

Gloria smiled; "That's exactly what I said, so hurry up and

get dressed while I fix you something to eat. Then, we're going to give your mom a surprise she'll never forget! So hurry!"

The kids started jumping up and down on the bed while yelling; "Yeah! Yeah! We're going to see mommy! Yeah!" Gloria walked out the room and into the kitchen to fix everyone some breakfast while the kids got dressed.

CHAPTER NINETEEN

It's the middle of the afternoon. Gloria and the kids are at the prison, waiting for La Vonne to arrive in the waiting area. As they wait, the children are antsy, excited to see their mother. They are nervous while watching the unfamiliar sights in the prison. They are also unsure about their feelings for their mother, due to the distance and circumstances of what she did. However, they are hopeful, allowing them to be excited about finally seeing their mom. Gloria is happy to see the joy in their eyes, but can tell that they are uncertain and nervous. Suddenly, a sound is heard as the door to the tiny room is opened by a key.

At the first sight of their mom, Jr. and Stacy scream with excitement, while running toward La Vonne. "Mommy! Mommy!" they say. Seeing their mother makes all uncertain or negative thought they had disappear. They're just happy to see her.

La Vonne stands in total shock as she looks at the innocent faces of her children. "Oh my God! Oh my God! My babies!" She tries not to cry. She bends down and holds her children like never before. She's so happy, yet she can't believe they're in the same room with her. Jr. and Stacy are very excited to finally see and hold their mother since she was taken away from them two years ago. Gloria sits back in the chair and enjoys the view.

La Vonne pulls the children away from her, then back into

Momma, Please Forgive Me!

her arms as she admires their looks and how much they've grown. Jr. has short black hair, medium brown skin and wears a big smile with pretty white teeth. He's wearing his favorite football jersey to impress his mom. Stacy has on her favorite *Barbie* tee-shirt and is carring her favorite black *Barbie* in her hands. She has long dark braids, dimples in her cheek and soft brown skin. She also has pearl earings in her ears and a necklace to match.

"Oh my God! I can't believe this. This is a miracle! This is the best miracle I've had since I came here. My babies are here! My babies are finally here to see me!" she said with excitement. Then she looks at her mom; "Thanks Momma for bringing my babies to see me."

Gloria looks at her and smiles; "You're welcomed baby. This is something I should have done a long time ago."

While La Vonne continues hugging her children she adds; "But you're here now and we can't change the past. So, thank you!" "You're so welcomed."

Then Stacy looks at her mother with a very serious expression on her face; "Are you alright?"

La Vonne takes her back into her arms and responds; "Yes baby, I'm alright. Especially now that you're here. But I'll be better when I come home to be with you guys."

Jr. looks at his mom with a confused look on his face and responds; "Mommy, when are you coming home?"

La Vonne sees the sadness in his eyes and tries to explain. "Honey, I don't know right now. Grandma is trying to help me. You see, I did a very bad thing when I killed your daddy and I'm very sorry for doing that. But at the time, I didn't know what I was doing. The only thing I was trying to do was make sure he didn't hurt us again. Now, I know that I should have handled things differently. So, as soon as I can prove to the judge that I'm not a bad person, I'll be able to come home with all of you."

Both of the kids had very serious looks on their faces while she explained. Gloria could see that they still weren't clear with La Vonne's explanation. Therefore, she added on to what La Vonne said; "Kids, don't worry. Grandma is going to do what she can to get your mom out of this place."

Jr. looked at La Vonne with a sad and confused look on his face. He was still trying to understand what was going on and why his mother couldn't come home with them now. "Mommy, I miss you. I want you to come home now!" Suddenly a few tears fell down his face.

La Vonne hugged him, trying to console him. "I miss you too baby. I'm trying really hard to come home as soon as I can, but it takes time. I hope you two will forgive me for taking your daddy away from you. I didn't mean to break up our family. I really didn't mean to do that." she said with pain.

Jr. looked at his mom, the pain in her eyes and felt sorry. "Mommy, I remember what dad did to you. I'll always remember what he did. I know he hurt you. He even hurt me. So I forgive you. I know you didn't mean to kill him, Grandma told us so."

La Vonne smiled and looked at Gloria; "Thank you Momma." Then she looked into the eyes of her babies; "Grandma is right. I didn't mean to kill him. I just didn't want him to ever hurt us again, that's all." Then she changed the tone to that of being pleasant and happy. "So, what have you two been up to lately. It's been a long time since I've seen both of you and I want to hear everything."

The children's solemn faces lit up as they prepared to catch their mother up on what was going on in their lives. "Mommy, I've been playing outside and going to school everyday." Stacy said with excitement.

La Vonne was happy to hear her comments because she didn't know if they would ever forgive her after what she had done to their father. She graciously welcomed their conversation with opened arms. "You have?" she said with the same excitement Stacy presented. "And what else have you been doing in school? Do you have a best friend?"

While La Vonne directed her statement to Stacy, Jr. interrupted; "She has a boyfriend," he teased. His statement made Stacy mad, causing her to defend her honor; "No I don't! Stop saying that! Grandma tell him to stop!"

Listening to Stacy's words made La Vonne sad. She wished that Stacy would have asked her to tell her brother to stop, instead of her asking Gloria. However, she knew that her children had grown to rely on Gloria for guidance, and not her. Those thoughts gave her a stronger desire to fight for her freedom. Gloria could see the hurt in La Vonne's eye, but remained silent and helpless, knowing that there was nothing she could do to change the way things were.

Suddenly La Vonne decided to take charge, reminding her children that she was still their mother and wanted to be in charge while they were in her presence. "Jr., be nice to your sister. Let her tell me about her school. Then I want to hear all about yours."

Stacy smiled, licked her tongue at her brother while he licked his back. Then she continued; "Well, I have a friend named Cathy. She's my best friend in the whole wide world. My teacher's name is Ms. Nancy. They're both nice."
Then La Vonne smiled and responded; "That's nice."

Then she looked at Jr.; "Now, tell me all about your teacher and friends." Jr. looked at Stacy, stuck his tongue out, looked at his mom and smiled. "Well, my best friend's name is Perry. He's in my class and we play at school all the time. My teacher's name is Ms. Kelly and she's real nice too." he said with pride and confidence.

Just at that moment, the good time came to an abrupt end when the guard interrupted; "Alright, visiting hours are up. Your guests have to leave now." His attitude was very confident and arrogant.

His tone frightened Stacy, causing her to grab a hold of La Vonne and cry; "Mommy, I don't want to leave you. Please Mr. Guard, can she come home with us? Please! Please!!" she pleaded to no avail.

As Gloria watched the pain and concern in Stacy's eyes, she began to re-evaluated her decision of bringing her grandchildren to the prison. Nevertheless, she knew that it was more important for them to be with their mom, reuniting them as a family.

La Vonne also felt Stacy's pain. She realized how hard all of this was for her to endure. Although, she knew that there was nothing she could do to ease her fears and concerns. "It's alright baby. I'll be home soon, I promise!" La Vonne was trying to console her daughter. Then she continued; "Grandma is going to help me. So go home and come back to visit me another day."

Jr. was worried and decided to add to the conversation; "Mommy, do we have to leave now? We just got here." Then he looked at the guard with a mean look and stuck out his lips, pouting.

The guard looked at Jr. with a stern look, and then addressed everyone in a demanding tone; "I said it's time to go!" There was no sympathy in his voice for anyone. "Tell your visitors to leave now or else!" He began hitting his billy club in his hand, looking at everyone with anger.

Gloria could see that their delay would only make it hard for La Vonne. She also knew that his tone was frightening the kids, causing her to take action. "Come on kids. We have to leave now. We don't want your mom to get in trouble." Then she looked at the guard with an evil eye and continued; "We'll come back to see her later, I promise. And remember, we're going to work real hard to bring your mom home soon."

Gloria and her grandchildren stood up and waved at

Momma, Please Forgive Me!

La Vonne. "Bye Mommy! Bye! I love you," Stacy said with tears slowly falling from her eyes.

"I love you too Mommy. Come home soon," Jr. said with a hurtful tone to his voice, while trying to be strong. Everyone stood in silence while the guard escorted La Vonne back to her cell, leaving the loud sound of the steel door closing and locking.

After La Vonne left the room, Gloria and her grandchildren cried out loud. They had been left all alone in the small and dreary room. Then, they slowly and quietly walked out and returned to their car.

After returning to the car, everyone had remained quiet. They were all thinking about the day and how things happened. "Grandma, are you really going to bring Mommy home soon?" Jr. said with a puzzled look on his face.

Gloria looked down at his sad and hollow eyes and responded; "Child, with God's help I sure am gonna bring your Mommy back home." Then they continued their walk to the car and went home. While taking the long drive home, the kids remained quiet. Gloria prayed in silence for God's help while she drove. She did not want her grandchildren to ever lose faith in her or her words of promise. "Lord please bring La Vonne home and ease the hurt feelings of my grandchildren."

CHAPTER TWENTY

It's late in the afternoon. Gloria is at home sitting at her kitchen table holding the telephone to her ear. "Office of Bethel Mitchell. How may I help you?" the voice of Jay's secretary says in response to the caller. "Yes, this is Gloria Johnson. I would like to speak to Mr. Mitchell please."

"One moment Miss Johnson. Let me see if he's available."

"Thank you, and tell him it's very important," Gloria quickly says before the secretary puts her on hold.

"Ok, hold on please." Then the secretary placed Gloria on hold and notifies Jay of the call. "Jay, I have Miss Gloria Johnson on the telephone, and she says that her matter is very important."

"Thank you Karen. I'll take her call." Then he picks up her call; "Hello Miss Johnson. How are you doing today? Is everything alright?" he says with concern.

Gloria responds with an upsetting tone; "No, everything is not alright."

"What's the problem?" he says with worry in his voice.

"It's my grandchildren! I took them to see La Vonne and they took the visit very hard. Jay, there has to be something you can do to get her out of there; there just has to be. I can't sit back and watch the hurt and pain in the eyes of these children each time they go to see their mom locked away in a prison."

Jay could clearly understand the hurt and concern Gloria shared with him. "Calm down, calm down. I was working on La Vonne's case when you called. Right now I'm going over all the information that the other lawyer had. However, in order for me to get another appeal date I have to find some new evidence. If I can't find any new evidence I'm afraid they won't hear her case," he said in a solemn tone.

Hearing his tone caused Gloria to worry. "Jay, when I first met you, you had high hopes of getting La Vonne freed. Are you telling me that now you don't think you can do that?"

Jay immediately defended his words; "Oh no! I'm not saying that at all! I still have faith in getting your daughter out of prison. However, it may take more time than I expected. Believe me, when I say that I will do all that I can to get your daughter out of prison, mark my word that I'll do just that. Remember, we have God on our side."

Suddenly Gloria smiled, calming down while feeling better after hearing Jay's words. "Yes we do. I just hope that God lets her get out soon. I would hate to watch the look in those precious little babies eyes after telling them that their mother will spend the rest of her life in prison. Jay, those words I hope I'll never have to say."

Jay smiled, knowing that he had helped ease Gloria's doubts. "Miss Johnson, I don't think those words will be anything you'll ever have to say. I truly believe that La Vonne will be freed. But like I said, it may take awhile because the courts are overbooked with cases, and she'll have to wait her turn before she's called back. You must not forget that she just saw a judge and was denied a release. So it may take awhile before another judge will hear her case, that is unless we come up with some new evidence. So, until then, stay in prayer and know that I'm doing all I can do in order to get her released. After I finish reviewing her files, I'll be in touch with you. Together, and with the help of God, we'll definitely come up with some kind of strategy to free her."

After listening to Jay's words, Gloria was feeling more hopeful. "Thank you Jay," she said with a big smile. "Thank you very much. I feel much better now. Bye," she said as she ended. "Bye Gloria." Gloria hangs up the phone and goes to check on her grandchildren.

CHAPTER TWENTY-ONE

Eight years have now passed and La Vonne is still in prison. During this long span La Vonne, Jay and Gloria continue their quest of getting her released from prison. They are waiting for something that will give them the needed ammunition that will grant her another appeal. While she awaits, she has endured more pain and heartache while anticipating the day that she'll be set free. She also becomes stronger, learning how to stay alive by defending herself and keeping some sort of sanity, while remaining a prisoner. Gloria has made sure that her grandchildren visit their mother regularly. As their visits increase, so does their faith that one day their mother will come home. Jr. is now sixteen years old and Stacy is fourteen.

It's late at night and La Vonne is trying to sleep through the hot summer temperatures. The output of the air conditioning in the prison is very low in order to conserve energy, making everyone uncomfortable. They have no other way to keep themselves cool, other than the paper fans that have become invaluable.

While laying in her bed, optimism is far from La Vonne's mind. She thought she would have been released a long time ago, but so far no new evidence has surfaced that would be strong enough, granting her a new appeal. As La Vonne lays on her bed fanning her heated body, Trina, who has been a prison guard for over twelve years, stops at her cell door while making her nightly rounds. La Vonne notices her walk bye and speaks; "Hey Trina."

Trina responds to the friendly greeting; "Hey girl. How you doing?"

Still feeling discouraged, La Vonne knew that she could confide in Trina. La Vonne also knew that Trina has always expressed positive and uplifting words, lifting her spirits, which she desperately needed to hear right now. "Girl, it's been ten long years and I'm still here. When am I ever going to get out of this place?"

Trina could feel her pain and felt sorry for her. "Girl, I feel you. I know you can't wait to get out of here, but keep the faith. After all this time, don't give up now. Especially after everything you've been through. If nothing else, hang in there for the sake of your kids. They're the ones who need you to be strong the most!"

Momma, Please Forgive Me!

Trina's words were already beginning to make La Vonne feel better. "Girl, I feel you. But I can't stand it in here!" she said with force in her voice. "I'll sure be glad when I can leave and go home to be with my family. But you're right, knowing that my children are waiting for me will make my wait sweeter when I do get out. I'm sure glad my mother has been bringing them to see me over the last eight years. Because facing the fact of being locked up, then not seeing them during the first two years of my term were the worst. I don't think I could have held on this long if they hadn't been coming all these years, or if they couldn't have forgiven me for killing their dad."

"See, so cheer up girl! By knowing that they're in your corner says a lot. Don't worry, you'll be out of this place soon enough! Just hang in there a little longer. Did you ever find some dirt on Jonathan?" Trina said as La Vonne continued in a depressed tone; "No, nothing yet. It seems that he kept his skeletons covered up so good that no one's talking. Everyone seems to be afraid of even mentioning his name."

Trina shook her head in disbelief; "Well, keep looking. Don't ever give up. Like I said a long time ago, that could be the one thing that could grant your freedom."

La Vonne felt a little better after talking to Trina. "Thanks for the pep talk, I sure needed it."

"You're welcomed. I gotta go now. Take care and be strong."

Trina walks away as La Vonne responds; "Thanks, I will. Bye." Trina waves as she continues her rounds checking each cell to make sure every prisoner was accounted for.

After Trina left, La Vonne laid back down when suddenly she heard someone whispering; "La Vonne. La Vonne. Are you still awake?" the mystery voice said.

"Yeah, I'm still awake. What's up?" La Vonne responded

to the voice of her next door cell mate Sherri. Sherri was leaning against her cell door towards La Vonne's door, trying to keep her voice to a whisper.

"I heard what you and Trina were talking about. I agree with you, you shouldn't be in this place. Hell, I wouldn't be in here if I hadn't done a stupid thing myself. But anyway, we ain't talking about me. But you on the other hand, should have been out of here a long time ago. So, what are you going to do now? How are you going to get out of here? Are you planning to make a run for it or what?" Sherri rattled with curiosity.

"Girl, I don't know what I'm gonna do. I'm still trying to figure something out. I miss my children so much. I want to be home with them so bad I can taste it. Right now my lawyer is doing everything he can. He's spoken to several members on the appeals board, but nothing seems to be good enough. He says that he needs some new evidence in order for me to be granted another appeal. So, right now I'm trying to find some dirt on my ex that will give me the evidence I need. If I can just prove that he could have harmed me and my kids, it would help my case. But first I have to prove to the judge that our lives were in danger. Even though I knew that we were in danger every time he walked in the door high on drugs or drunk, smelling like a liquor bottle, is not enough. The judge needs solid proof. My word is not good enough to get released or get another appeal."

"That's all you need is some new evidence? Girl, that should be easy."

La Vonne felt bad. She thought that finding new evidence would be easy, but she was wrong. "Well, so far, that's something that hasn't happened. All I know is that I have to think of something fast if I'm ever going to get out of here and be with my children again."

"Well, keep thinking." Sherri was trying to cheer La Vonne

up. "I'm sure you'll think of something that dirty bastard did that would grant you an appeal. I wish finding some new evidence was all I needed to get me out of here. But I've got another six years before that will happen. All I can say about my situation is, me trying to kill that son-of-a-bitch, screwing-ass, motha' fucka ex-boyfriend of mine, Sonny, was well worth it!"

La Vonne looked confused hearing Sherri's words. They were words Sherri never spoke about in the past. Then she continued; "Hell, I'd do it again if I had to! That's what he deserved for messing around on me, trying to make me look like a damn fool. Girl, it seems that the more you do for a nigga', the more they take you for granted! And I did everything I could to please his black ass, and he repaid me by sleeping with my best friend, not once, but for two whole months, and then the bitch got pregnant! Hell, he already had two kids by me and didn't take care of em', so why did he feel he needed another one from my best friend? That bastard and bitch, I should have killed both of their asses! Some best friend she was, sleeping with my man while I was out working like a dog, trying to keep food on our table, while his lazy ass screwed her during the day and then hung out all damn night with his friends. Because of that shit, I'll never have a best friend again. But in the end, I got the last laugh!"

La Vonne couldn't believe what she was hearing, but kept her ear glued to every word as Sherri continued; "Girl, I came home from work early one day and found them sleep in my bed, laying all butt naked on my bed with smiles on their faces. Can you believe that shit! They were sleep in my damn bed, the one I bought with my damn money! Hell, I creeped to the hall closet and got my 45 and I tried to blow both of theie asses away while they laid there sleep. Girl, you should have seen her run her naked ass out my house after the first shot went off, but Sonny, he wasn't so lucky. I shot his dick right off from his balls! Now, he's a crippled, dickless bastard!

And home girl is lucky that my sister was with me, because she grabbed the gun out of my hand before I could get to her ass, because I was going to kill her after I finished with him." Then Sherri laughed while explaining her story. "Girl, you should have seen her. That bitch was so scared that she peed on herself as she ran her naked ass out my house. Now, I want to see him or her try to mess around on somebody else. They might not be so lucky the next time."

Then La Vonne and Sherri both laughed; "Girl you're crazy! I thought I was crazy, but you beat me out by a mile. Believe me, I do know the feeling. Sometimes you just have to do what you have to do. But I wish I hadn't killed Jonathan. I wish he would have killed himself instead of me doing. Because the way he was living, it would have been a matter of time before he would have been dead anyway! You see, if I hadn't done it, somebody else surly would have, especially since he was hooked on those drugs. Then I could have been like a faire tale, happily ever after with just me and my kids. But what can I say? At the time I thought I was doing the right thing, now I know I didn't. Too bad I can't turn back the hands of time. I've learned to realize that it's just something I have to get used to and hope for the best."

"Yeah, I know." Sherri said. "Believe me, I know. Hey La Vonne?"
"Yeah?"

"Who did your ex hang out with anyway? I might know somebody who knew him. Because my ex did those damn drugs too, and you know all those bastard's hung in the same circle. And since we didn't live too far away from each other, they may have known each other."

La Vonne held on to Sherri's every word while also thinking out loud about Jonathan's past. "I do know that Jonathan hung out with Billy Ray and Cool Joe. Toward the end, he also hung out with Smokey and Donald. And since Sonny did drugs, he probably knew Smokey and Donald. Hell, those two bastard's were the biggest drug dealers in town. They sold shit to everybody. They also had several people working for them. As far as I know Jonathan could have been one of their biggest dealers, because they didn't let too many people get too close to their circle. I heard they even had guys from the police department working for them. I can imagine that their association with the cops allowed them to pass their drugs in even larger circles."

Sherri began thinking out loud; "You know, now that you mention it, Sonny probably did know those guys. Let me think. I do remember him mentioning somebody named Smokey and Donald a few times. But I never paid to much attention to what he said about what he was doing. I was always busy with the kids."

La Vonne began to get excited with the possibility of a connection that could be the answer she needed; "Girl, those two brothers were the biggest drug pushers in town. Our ex's had to know those fools since they were all doing the same thing. Think girl, think!"

Suddenly Sherri's memory came alive; "Girl you're right!" The tone in Sherri's voice triggered La Vonne's eyes to grow large with hope, as she continued to listen. "Now that you mention it, I do remember seeing those fools around my house. In fact, I may have seen your ex with them one day. It was one night after a party Sonny went to. I was sleep, when all of a sudden I heard my front door slam loud. That shit woke me up and made the kids start crying."

"What happened?" La Vonne said with anticipation as she continued to hold on to Sherri's every word. "Let me think. Oh yeah!"

"What? What?" La Vonne said with suspense as Sherri continued; "Well, after I heard the door slam, I looked out the window and saw two guys in a car and another one in the backseat. I couldn't see the one in the backseat too good because it was dark outside. But I do remember that after Sonny came in the house, those fools were outside saying that they were going to kick his ass if he told anybody what happened."

"Go on, what happened next? What happened?" La Vonne said with anxiety.

Sherri continued; "Girl, I don't know exactly what happened. Because Sonny was so mad that he refused to talk about it. He just told me that it wasn't any of my business and to just forget what I heard. Then he went to sleep with the gun by his side. But after he fell asleep the nigga' started talking."

La Vonne was really on edge now; "Go ahead. Keep talking."

"Anyway, the nigga' started talking in his sleep and that tripped me out. He started saying shit like Jonathan killed somebody and he had to get back home. He kept saying something about not wanting to go back to prison for that nigga'."

Hearing Sherri's words completely astonished La Vonne, almost leaving her speechless. However, she found the words to respond; "Killed somebody? Girl, go on! What else did he say after that? Think hard, you may be able to help me get out of here. Think!"

Sherri continued; "He kept saying something about a dude named Jonathan killed somebody and he had to get the fuck home. I guess he didn't want to go to prison for something somebody else did, especially since he already had two strikes against him and was on parole. He knew that if he went to prison again, he wasn't coming out. So he wanted no part of whatever this Jonathan guy had done."

After hearing the news, La Vonne began feeling hopeful. "Is that all he said? Did he say who Jonathan killed? Or the location

Momma, Please Forgive Me!

of where he killed the person at? Think Sherri, this could be the very thing that can get me out of here. Especially if this is my Jonathan Sonny was talking about."

"Girl, slow down. Let me think, cause that was over eleven years ago." Sherri continued to think while La Vonne continued to talk. "Girl, when Jonathan was high on those drugs, killing somebody would've been easy for him to do. Those drugs made him so angry that no one could cross him the wrong way. He was stone out of his mind when he was high, and during that time he stayed high all the time."

Suddenly Sherri's memory was triggered again; "Oh yeah, I remember now."

"What? What do you remember?" La Vonne anxiously said as Sherri continued; "Well, after you killed Jonathan, I do remember Sonny showing me Jonathan's picture in the newspaper. Then he said something about 'that nigga' deserved everything he got! Because if she didn't kill him, somebody else sure would have.' Then he started laughing and said; 'that's a damn shame that his family never found all the money he'd stashed away from his drug deals, because they were too poor to bury him and his wife was locked away in prison. So that nigga's body must be buried in some city dump. But no body cared about him anyway. He didn't have any real friends. The only friends he had were the ones he sold too. I guess that's why no body bothered to go to his so-called funeral.' Then he stopped talking, and that's all I can remember."

After hearing what Sherri had to say, La Vonne was very happy. "Thanks Sherri! This may be the very answer I've been looking for. This information could help set me free!"

"So, what you gonna do now?"

La Vonne was still thinking out loud; "Well first of all, I'm gonna tell my lawyer what you said so that he can check out your story. Because if Jonathan did kill somebody, it'll prove that he was capable of killing me and my kids. It would justify my actions against him and maybe get me out of this damn place."

Sherri was happy she could help. "Well, good luck girl. I feel for you. I just hate that I'm stuck in this damn place for another six years. I wish that finding out dirt on my ex was all I needed to get out of here. But what I did was intentional. I was aiming for his black ass. So nothing like that will work for me. Maybe in a few years I'll get out early for good behavior."

"Yeah, that's true." La Vonne hoped the best for Sherri. She didn't wish for anyone to be locked up where she was. "Hey, if everything you told me works out, I don't plan on being here too much longer. And just maybe, your lead will look good in the eyes of the judge as well to help me with an early release. Well, we better get some sleep. And if you think of something else, wake me up and let me know."

"Will do." Sherri walked toward her bed; "Goodnight."

Then La Vonne walked back to her bed and laid down; "Goodnight and thanks again."

"No problem. Anything for a fellow sista'." Sherri added before she rolled over and fell asleep.

La Vonne laid in her bed with a smile on her face. She now had hope of soon becoming free.

CHAPTER TWENTY-TWO

It's nine o'clock in the morning and the day is bright. Jay's feeling like today is his lucky day, but he doesn't know why. His office hasn't been opened very long when the telephone rings; "Law offices of Bethel Mitchell. Can I help you?" his secretary responds to the caller.

An operator is on the other line and responds; "Will you

Momma, Please Forgive Me!

accept a collect call from La Vonne Brown?"

The secretary responds; "Yes Operator, put the call through." Then the operator connects the calls.

La Vonne is very anxious; "Hello, can I speak to Mr. Mitchell please, it's very important. Is he there?" she says without taking a breathe.

"Just one moment please Ms. Brown. I'll connect you."

Jay picks up the phone; "Hello La Vonne. How can I help you?" La Vonne is so excited that she can hardly contain her information.

"Hello Jay. I have some new information that might help my case. In fact, if it's true, it'll definitely help my case."

Jay was puzzled, but curious as to what she had to say. "What kind of information?"

"Well, last night I was talking to my cell-mate and she told me that Jonathan may have killed somebody. Is there any way you can find out if this information is true or not? Couldn't this be the new evidence I need to get me out of here?" she said as she barely took breathes in between her sentences.

Jay was happy with her information. "Yes, this could be exactly what you need. Who told you this information?"

"Her name is Sherri. She's a real cool sister. She stays in the cell next to mine. She got in here shortly after me."

This news excited Jay. He wanted La Vonne to be released as bad as she wanted her freedom. "I'll tell you what. I'll come down there later today and find out all the details. Then, we'll take it from there. I'll also bring your mom. She may know some of the contacts to verify Sherri's story."

La Vonne was happy that things were taking a positive direction and smiled like there was no tomorrow. "I'll be waiting! Thanks."

"No problem. I'll see you soon."

"Ok!" La Vonne responded in a flirtatious way. Then, they hung up their telephones and La Vonne walked back to her cell feeling happy and content.

It's mid-afternoon. Jay and Gloria are waiting for La Vonne in the prison's meeting room. Everyone's excited about the news that could possibly set La Vonne free. As La Vonne walks into the room, a big smile fills her face; "Hi," she says as she walks over to Gloria and hugs her.

Jay stands to greet La Vonne; "Hello La Vonne." Then he shakes her hand and sits back down.

"Hi Jay." she said blushing, hoping that something more than business would come out of their union. Then La Vonne sat down and looked at Gloria. "Hi Momma."

Gloria responds with a big smile on her face. "Hi Baby. How are you doing?"

"I'm feeling much better now. I think the information Sherri told me last night will help me a whole lot. This could be the very thing that can get me out of here."

"Baby I'm so happy for you."

Jay was ready to get right to work, so he quickly cut into their conversation; "Now, tell me everything Sherri told you. And don't leave anything out of the story," Jay instructed La Vonne.

La Vonne began to discuss the details while Jay took notes with his tape recorder and Gloria listened carefully. After a half an hour, La Vonne was finished; "And that's everything she told me."

"Ok, are you sure that's it? You didn't leave anything out did you?" Jay said.

La Vonne shook her head; "No, I didn't leave anything out. That's everything."

Gloria added her two cents; "Did Sherri say if Sonny was still alive or is he dead?"

La Vonne looked unsure; "I think he's still alive. She didn't say he was dead. But she did say that he was crippled now. She also said that they didn't stay too far away from where we used to live. Hopefully he's still in the area."

While Jay listened, he came up with a strategy; "If he still lives in your old neighborhood, that'll make things easier. I'll try to find out what I can pull from his police files. Gloria, you start asking around the neighborhood, or look for some of La Vonne's old friends. See if any of them know where this Sonny is and if he's still alive. La Vonne, did you get his last name?" La Vonne had a puzzled look on her face. "No I didn't."

Then Jay continued; "Well, that will be your job. When you go back to your cell. Ask Sherri what his last name is. Then call my office with the information. I'll tell my secretary to expect your call. Miss Johnson, can you handle your job?"

Gloria stuck out her chest, smiled and responded; "Yes I can! La Vonne, where's your old telephone book?"

La Vonne scratched her head and thought for a moment; "It's probably stored away in your garage with all my other things."

"Ok, I'll look through that stuff when I get home. Would the kids know what it looks like?"
"Jr. would."

Gloria was now ready to go to work. "Good, then I'll have him help me find it. Then, I'll start calling some of your old friends and see what they know. Hopefully, they still remember who you are, because it has been over ten years since anyone has heard from you."

La Vonne looked at Gloria and smiled; "I know it's been awhile, but I sure hope someone still remembers who I am. I also hope someone still has the same telephone number, because it has been ten years and people do move on. Anyway, thank you Momma for helping and thank you too Jay."

Jay put his tape recorder away; "Ok, so now we all know

what we have to do. La Vonne, once we find out more information, I'll be in touch."

La Vonne felt good about the plan; "Ok, I'll call your office right away."

Jay smiled; "That sounds like a winner. It's good that Sherri told you all that information. It's too bad she didn't tell you sooner."

La Vonne smiled and responded; "That's true, but we can't turn back time. At least now I have more hope of getting out of here than I ever had before. And that's the best news I've had in ten years."

Gloria looked up to God, raised her hands and said out loud; "Praise the Lord!" Then she looked at La Vonne; "I knew God would see you through all of this mess. He told me he would and I believe that his will, will be done."

La Vonne hugged Gloria and looked her in the eye; "Thank you Momma for everything. Your forgiveness is why I have another chance. Thank you for forgiving me." Then La Vonne looked at Jay; "Jay, I also want to thank you for believing in me. I wish I had you on my side from the beginning. Because if I did, I don't think I would still be in here now."

"Thank you. Now, everybody get to work and lets get you freed!" La Vonne hugged Jay and Gloria tightly while successfully holding back her tears.

****

It's late in the afternoon. Gloria has made it back home. She changes her dress clothes into some old clothes. Then she gets Jr. to come to the garage and help her look for La Vonne's telephone book. The garage is still hot from the afternoon sun and from being locked up for so many years without any visitors. There

Momma, Please Forgive Me!

are spider webs throughout the garage. La Vonne's belongings are stacked to the ceiling, leaving very little room to walk. Jr. and Gloria look at the boxes in the garage, then look at each other and frown. However, they take a deep breath and do what was needed to do in order to free La Vonne.

While they look through the boxes with no luck, time quickly passes by, changing the sun-setting daylight into nightfall. The nightfall has caused the dimly lit garage to become harder for them to see, causing them to work faster.

"Jr. we have to hurry because once it gets darker, we won't be able to see a thing in here. The light is much too dim to see with all of these boxes stacked so high. And tomorrow you have to go to school and I won't know what I'm looking for."

Jr. looked at the boxes, then at his grandmother; "Grandma, do we have to look through all of these boxes tonight? Can't we look tomorrow?"

Gloria looked at him with a very disappointed and stern look on her face. "Yes, we have to look through all these boxes tonight! Now, get to looking, instead of complaining! We need to find your mother's phone book today so we can get her freed from prison as soon as possible. Jr. think about it like this, when you're locked away from everyone, everyday adds up to a lifetime of frustration and pain. And we don't want your mom to go through any more pain than she needs to go through. So, keep looking. One day I'll get a better light for this garage. But for now, lets hurry!"

Jr. wanted his mother freed, but he didn't want to look through all of those dirty boxes. He had a very sad look on his face which projected a somber tone; "Ok Grandma." Then they continued looking through the boxes.

After searching for a few hours, Jr. had an excited tone to his voice; "I found it! Here it is!" He said as he held up La Vonne's little black phone book.

Gloria's face lit up with joy as she went to the spot where the book was found. "Good, now we can go inside and get out of this dirty garage and get on some clean clothes." Jr. left, leaving Gloria alone to lock the garage.

After taking a shower and putting on some clean clothes, Gloria sat down at the kitchen table and looked through the book. As she looked, she called some of the numbers that were listed, starting with the letter A. "Hello, is La Shawn Anderson home?" Gloria said to the first caller she attempted.

The person on the other end responded; "Lady, you have the wrong number. Nobody lives here named La Shawn."

"Thank you." Gloria said, hanging up, feeling sad.

However by knowing what she had to do, she gained her composure and continued her search, making several other calls. As she continued her quest, an hour passed with still no luck. Her efforts were beginning to cause her to feel weary and tired. Just when Gloria was ready to give up, her luck changed. "Hello, is Peaches Sanford home?" Gloria asked the voice on the other end. The person responded; "This is her, who's this?"

After hearing the response, Gloria's face lit up with joy and excitement. "Hi, my name is Gloria Johnson. I'm La Vonne Brown's mother."

"Hi Miss Johnson. Its been a long time. How's La Vonne doing?"

"She's fine."

"Is she still in prison?"

Gloria's response was sad; "Yes, I'm afraid she is." Then her response became happy; "But I'm working hard to get her out of that filthy place."

Peaches felt hopeful hearing the news. "I heard that!" she said with excitement. "You know Miss Johnson, I never thought they would actually lock La Vonne up. Especially after

Momma, Please Forgive Me!

those who knew how Jonathan treated her testified on her behalf. And just think, he was so nice when she married him. I used to visit them all the time in the beginning. There wasn't anything he wouldn't do for La Vonne. He loved her and she loved them, they were inseparable. And Lord God, when Jr. was born, boy was that a happy day for both of them. Jonathan couldn't stop smiling. He wouldn't even let La Vonne walk by herself or go anywhere, because he didn't want her to hurt herself of their baby. However things changed and no one really knew how bad things had changed until it was too late. La Vonne covered everything up so well. We knew that they would argue. But we never knew he was beating her. I guess on those days, she wouldn't answer the phone or the door, so no one really knew that things had gotten so bad. It's too bad that the testimony we did have wasn't good enough to let her go. That was such a shame. I felt so bad after they sentenced her. You make sure to tell her that I said hi. And tell her that I hope she gets out soon! Oh my God, I've been running my mouth so much that I never asked you what you called for. Does La Vonne need anything? Is there anything I can do to help her?"

Gloria smiled and responded; "As a matter of fact there is something you can do to help."

Peaches was anxious to hear her request; "Just name it. La Vonne was my girl. If there's anything I can do to help her, you can count on me. So, what can I do to help?"

Hearing Peaches' response made Gloria so happy. She knew that now she would be able to go forth with La Vonne's case. Gloria told Peaches the entire story while she carefully listened.

After Gloria finished her story, she waited for Peaches' response. She hoped for the best; "So, what do you think? Do you think you can find some information on this Sonny person?"

Peaches was more than happy to help. "Sure I can! I never

liked that punk anyway. In fact, I know someone who used to hang out with Sonny. I used to see him all the time. But I haven't seen him around the neighborhood in a long while. I haven't even heard his name mentioned around town. Hopefully nobody killed him, because I agree that his story can help La Vonne. That guy was never up to any good. Anybody he hung out with was bad news. People knew not to mess with him or anybody he hung out with. So, if he's still alive, I'll find him for you. Give me your telephone number and I'll call you as soon as I find something out."

Hearing Peaches' words were music to Gloria's ears. She felt very hopeful of getting La Vonne freed. "Thanks Peaches. You've been a very big help, especially since a lot of people don't want to get involved. But thank you for helping. I'll wait for your call."

"No problem. Like I said, La Vonne was my girl. I'll do whatever I can to help her. So, as soon as I hear anything I'll give you a call. Bye Miss Johnson. It was really nice to hear from you."

"You too Peaches. Bye and thank you." Gloria said as they hung up their telephones.

****

The night is very late. Everyone's asleep at Gloria's house, when suddenly Jr. begins tossing and turning in his bed. He's having a nightmare. As he sleeps, he can visualize the entire fight that lead to the horrifying moments of his parents fatal fight. It also brings back memories of his father knocking him down and calling him a sissy. Ultimately, the violence lead to the death of his father by his mother, changing everyone's life for ever.

"Stop hitting her right now!" Jr. yelled out in his sleep. "Motha' fucka', I said stop hitting her right now or it's gonna be me and you! And be assured that I'm gonna kick your ass if you

Momma, Please Forgive Me!

hit her one more time! Then we'll see who's the real sissy after I kick your ass." he yelled out in furry.

The yelling suddenly woke Gloria up from her sleep, causing her to quickly run to his room. "Wake up baby, it's alright," she said while trying to shake him awake. "Wake up Jr. Grandma's here. Wake up now!" she repeated while holding him close in her arms.

He immediately woke up sweating and in a daze, then he looked around the room, fearing the worst; "Where is he? Where's he at? I'm gonna kick his ass. Where's he at?"

Gloria was blown away by his language. He spoke words she had never heard come out of his mouth before. However, she understood his anger, ignored his words and continued to hold him as tight as she could. She wanted to assure him that no more harm would come to him or his sister. "It's alright baby. It's gonna be alright. You must remember that your dad has been gone for a long time. He can never come back to hurt you or your mom again." In between his anger, Jr. looked into her eyes and tried to calm down, shaking away her hugs. "Baby, you have to remember that your dad can't ever hurt you ever again, I promise!" Gloria said while trying to hold him again.

"I'm alright Grandma. Thanks for caring. I know he can't come back, so why do I keep having these dreams? Why won't they just go away? I should have gotten over it all by now. Why do they keep coming back and why did he call me a sissy? Did he think that I was a sissy because I cried?" Then he looked directly into Gloria's eyes, waiting for an answer. Looking at the concern and hurt in his eyes, almost made her cry.

However, she kept her composure in order to give him the strength he needed to get through. "Oh God no child!" she said with anger. "Boy's are not sissy's because they cry. Sometimes they need to cry. Besides, after the way your daddy treated all of you, how could he expect for you to not cry? Jr., you must remember that your daddy only said those things because he wasn't himself."

Jr. looked at Gloria with his big brown eyes and continued to wonder as she continued. "You know, it's the one's who do cry, that feel better. If you always keep your feelings bottled up inside, that's when things can't get better. Sometimes crying helps. You must remember that men cry sometimes too, and that doesn't make them sissy's. I'm sure your daddy has cried before. You just may have not seen him do it. So, don't ever think that you're a sissy because you cried from the hurt your daddy put on you and your mom when you were a small child. You must also remember that you were only eight years old when all of that happened.
Now you're eighteen, almost a grown man and definitely not a sissy."

Jr. looked at his grandmother and smiled; "Thanks Grandma." Gloria smiled back and continued sharing her wisdom. "Try to go back to sleep and forget about that night. Everything is alright now, and when your mom gets out of prison, everything will really be alright, ok?" She looked at him to see if her words had helped. He looked back at her to assure her thoughts; "Ok."

However, she still wasn't sure if her words were enough. "Jr., do you want to talk to Pastor George again? His talks helped you when you were younger. I'm sure they can help now."

"No thanks. I'll be alright. I'm fine, really, I'm fine." Gloria was unsure with his decision. "Are you sure? I'm sure Pastor wouldn't mind."

"Really Grandma, I'm fine. Like you said, I'm almost a grown man. I'll get over it."
"If you say so."
"I say so."

"Ok then, well, go back to sleep. You have to go to school

in the morning."

He got back under his blankets and smiled; "I love you Grandma."

Gloria looked at his innocence and felt sorry. Even though he was grown, he was still a baby in her eyes. "I love you to baby. Goodnight."

"Goodnight," he responded as he turned over and quickly fell back to sleep. Gloria kissed him on his forehead, smiled and walked back to her room.

CHAPTER TWENTY-THREE

It's early in the morning and Jay is in his office talking on the telephone. During his conversation he's smiling and shaking his head in agreement with the caller. After he hangs up, he begins talking to himself out loud; "Yes! Yes! I found him!" Then he grabs his coat and briefcase and runs out of his office in search of Sonny Waters.

After driving for about thirty minutes, Jay has arrived on the other side of town, considered as the ghetto. The area is old, run down, potholes throughout the roads, old and inexpensive cars driving through the neighborhood and kids playing on the street corners with no where else to go. Jay is driving in a shiny black BMW. His fancy car is getting the attention of everyone within his view. It's also getting the attention of the white police officer who's sitting in his car parked across the street.

Jay slowly drives pass the policeman, who's observing his every move. Although the officer does nothing, he watches Jay closely, ready to make a move if necessary. Jay finally approaches the house he's been looking for and slows down. The house looks run-down, old and deserted. There's no grass in the front yard, only weeds surrounding the entire area. Many of the windows are broken with boards keeping them closed. Nevertheless, Jay stops his car and gets out. He's nervous, but makes an attempt toward the door with caution. After reaching the front door, he knocks. He stands there for approximately four minutes with no response coming from within.

Then, just as he turns to walk away someone comes to the closed door and yells; "Who is it?" the voice says with a curious tone. Jay stops in his tracks and turns back. He can not see the person behind the door because they're looking through the peep hole. The voice is that of an elderly woman.

"Hello. I'm looking for Sonny Waters. Does he live here?" Jay asked.

The mystery lady refuses to open the door, but answers; "Sometimes. But he's not here right now. He's probably at that damn church."

"What church?"

"The one up the street. His so-called new family, that's where. Now, quit bothering me. I'm watching my soap opera."

Jay takes what little information he can get and is happy. "Thank you," he says while hearing no other response. The voice is gone, leaving Jay at the porch alone. Then he gets in his car and drives away.

As he slowly drives down the street, he looks for any church that may lead him to Sonny. After driving a short distance, he discovers the only church on the block, surrounded by several liquor stores. The church is very large, with many empty parking spaces.

Jay pulls his car in the lot and parks. He attempts to get out when his cell phone rings. He stays put and answers; "Hello, this is Jay." He says, trying to rush the caller.

"Jay, this is Gloria Johnson. I have some news on that Sonny fellow." she says with excitement.

Momma, Please Forgive Me!

Gloria's tone causes Jay to also become excited. "That's good because I'm following a lead on him right now. What did you find out?"

"Believe it or not, he's a minister."

"A minister? After hearing all of what Sherri told La Vonne that definitely surprises me. So, where is he suppose to be a minister at, and I wonder if he's even a real minister, or if he's just covering up for his crimes." Jay said with suspicion.

"You got me. But one of La Vonne's friends called me this morning. She told me that she heard he's changed his lifestyle and is now preaching at a church close to his house."

Jay pulled down his sunglasses and looked at the church where he was parked. "Is it a Church of God in Christ by any chance?" he said with curiosity.

Gloria became excited after hearing his response; "Yeah! That's what Peaches said. How did you know?"

Jay summed up the large church and responded; "I just left his house and some strange lady, who never opened the door told me that I could find him at a church down the street. I'm at a church that fits that description right now. I'll call you back if I find him. If he did turn his life around, that would make La Vonne's case much stronger, especially if he has any information on Jonathan killing someone. So, I'll call you later. And thanks for the information."

Then Gloria smiled from ear to ear; "You're welcomed. I told you that getting my daughter out of that place is all I'm praying for and God will definitely see us through. So, call me as soon as you can."

Jay was now in a hurry to find out about Sonny. "I will, bye."

"Bye." Gloria said while Jay quickly hung up his telephone and made his way toward the church's office.

"Knock, knock, knock," were the sounds Jay made at the door of the office. A faint voice responded; "Who is it?"

"Hello, I'm looking for Sonny Waters," Jay responded. Suddenly the door opened automatically. Behind the door was Sonny Waters, sitting in a wheelchair. Jay was taken by surprise by what he saw as Sonny wheeled himself closer to Jay, welcoming him into the room.

"Come in. I'm Sonny Waters," he said with a smile on his face.

Jay walked into the room and looked around. There was a large picture of a black Jesus on one wall. On another wall was a small picture of Sonny, along with a few other men who were some of the church's associate pastors. After Jay walked in, Sonny shook Jay's hand rolled his wheelchair back behind the desk, where he was working before Jay arrived.

"Hello Mr. Waters. My name is Jay Mitchell. I'm the attorney representing La Vonne Brown." Jay said with confidence.

However, the name did not ring a bell with Sonny. "La Vonne Brown, that name sounds familiar. Who is she? Do I know her?" he said with a puzzled look on his face.

"I don't think you know her. She's a cell-mate to your ex-girlfriend Sherri."

Suddenly the puzzled look disappeared from Sonny's face. "The Lord has allowed me to forgive her. How's Sherri doing?" he said with a smile.

"I think she's fine." Jay said while trying to cut through the chase and get directly to the information he had come to get. "Anyway, La Vonne told me that you may have known her late husband, Jonathan Brown. Did you know him?" Jay asked, hoping for the best.

After hearing Jonathan's name, Sonny frowned. "Yeah, I knew him. I remember him very well. He was something else. It's

Momma, Please Forgive Me!

funny because I actually felt sorry for the guy after he got killed. Now I know where I heard that name, La Vonne. Wasn't she his wife? Wasn't she also the one who killed him?"

Sonny looked at Jay for answers as Jay explained; "Yes she is." Jay was trying not to focus on the negative situation by moving right along. "Now Mr. Waters, La Vonne said Sherri told her that you might have some very valuable information that could help set her free. I believe she shouldn't have ever went to prison in the first place. I personally think she got a bad rap."

Sonny was a little puzzled as to why La Vonne was still locked away. "I didn't know she was still in prison. I also agree that she should have never went to prison. From what I heard, she was the victim in the situation. During that time Jonathan wasn't a very nice person. When I first met him and before he lost his job, he was very nice. He used to always talk about his wife and kids and how much he loved them. But after losing his job he started selling drugs to keep food on the table. After that, his life changed for the worst, making him into a complete monster. In fact, during that time I wasn't such a good person myself. The drugs, money and women we became accustomed to changed all of us into monsters. However, after my accident I saw things differently, which caused me to change my bad habits. Now, I live for God."

Jay realized that Sonny knew Jonathan personally. Jay became happy, knowing that he was finally getting somewhere. He also knew that now his visit was actually going to pay off big time. "Can you tell me anything about Jonathan possibly killing someone. Do you know anything about that?" Jay held his breath, hoping for the answer he needed.

Sonny held his head down on the desk and shook it back and forth. "Yeah I do," he said with frustration and disappointment. Then, he continued; "But I was never sure about the full details. I heard several stories. But shortly after it happened I got shot. So, after recovering from my gunshot wound and going through all the long hours of therapy, I got away from everybody in that circle. I had to make a positive change in my life before I came up dead. I guess in a crazy way Sherri saved my life. Because if I had continued living the way I was living, I probably wouldn't be here today myself."

Jay became overjoyed in hearing the news. "Tell me what you do know? And can I tape your story?" he said with anticipation.

"Sure, you can tape me. I have nothing to hide anymore." Then Sonny proceeded with the story while Jay smiled, sat back and listened. "One night me and some of my boyz' were out partying and getting high. All of a sudden this brother got into Jonathan's face and accused him of sleeping with his woman, which he probably did. Anyway, Jonathan and this guy had some words. Then they started fighting. As the fight continued, Jonathan pulled out a knife and stabbed the guy. The guy fell down to the ground and died right on the spot. Well, the guys who I was with were all on probation, including me. So, going to prison for Jonathan was out of the question for all of us."

As Sonny talked, Jay became more excited, knowing that this was the exact thing that could help free La Vonne. Then Sonny continued; "So, all of us guys looked at each other and grabbed the dead body. We threw the body in the trunk of my boyz' car and we all jumped in and took off. I told them to take me home because I wasn't going to prison for something someone else did. So, they took me home and swore me to silence."

Jay was so excited about hearing the story that he could barely stay in his seat or contain the excitement blaring all over his face. "Did you ever tell anyone?" Jay asked.

"Not for a long time. But after I became a minister I decided to tell the police so I could clear my conscience."

Jay desperately reacted; "What did the police do? Did

Momma, Please Forgive Me!

they investigate or anything?"

Sonny responded with an uneasy tone; "I don't know. All I know is that I told them what I knew. Then I was cleared to leave. Ever since then, I've gone on with my life and never looked back."

Jay was blown away from his response. "Hmm, do you know who you talked to? Was a police report taken?"

"No, I never got the detective's name. All I knew was that he couldn't do anything without a dead body. You see, the man's body was never found. So, without a body, you can't prove anything." Sonny confessed.

"That was it? After hearing your statement they didn't do an investigation into finding the dead body?"

Sonny shook his head in agreement and held it down on the desk. Then looked up with a sad look in his eye; "I'm not sure what they did. But from what the detective said, I doubt if they did anything. Like I said earlier, all he was concerned about was knowing that another brother was off the streets. Then he started laughing. All I could do at the time was pray for the cop. Then I left the station, knowing that I did my part. I was just happy that he didn't lock me up for withholding or reporting information when the event actually took place. I just wanted to clear my conscience. Anyway, like I said, I did my part and thought they would handle the rest."

Jay looked at Sonny and then around the room with a dumbfounded look on his face. "Did you ever hear what happened to the body? This information could free an abused woman."

Sonny looked at Jay feeling sorry; "I'm sorry. I never looked back or asked any questions. With the guys we used to hang with, the less you knew, the better off you were," he said with shame.

Jay understood Sonny's reasons because he was a black man himself. He reflected back to the days when he wasn't able to afford a fancy car, or have money in the bank in order to live well in the American society. He knew how those days often made it hard to survive as a black man. He also knew that by being a black man living in America, didn't always allow you the breaks you needed in order to get ahead. Therefore, many felt they had to do what was necessary in order to survive. That way of thinking often forced those who didn't have, to acquire the better things in life the best way they could, normally by selling drugs.

"Is there anyway you can find out more information for me?" Jay asked with great desperation. "A woman and her children would be very grateful if you did."

Sonny looked at the expression on Jay's face and knew within his heart that he owed it to himself and to God to make things better if he could. "Hold on, let me make a call. I stay in touch with a few of my old friends who have made positive changes in their lives. They may know something." Then Sonny picked up the telephone, called someone and began talking about the murder. After talking to his friend for about ten minutes, Sonny hung up the telephone and had a stern and somber look on his face. "Ok, this is what I heard. But after I tell you this, the rest is up to you. I don't want any part of that life again." Jay was again happy to get any information he could. Therefore he was opened to any bargains he could make; "Ok, I'm listening. Go on," he said with anxiety.

Then Sonny continued; "My partner just told me that the body was buried in an opened grave. It's located in a field behind the baseball diamond at the park. The park is in the same neighborhood where we all lived. It's stashed somewhere at the bottom of the hill. That's all I know. So, it's on you now."

Jay looked at Sonny with an encouraged look; "Thank you very much! I'll take it from here. And thank you again for your time Mr. Waters. I may need to use your testimony in court, is that alright?" Jay hoped he wouldn't object.

Momma, Please Forgive Me!

"I have God on my side now. I'm not afraid of what any man can do to me. So call me if you need me." Sonny said with a smile on his face.

After hearing the news, Jay packed his belongings and prepared for his next mission of freeing La Vonne. "Thank you again. You've been a very big help. You have a nice day and I'll be in touch." Jay said while extending his hand out to shake Sonny's.

Sonny returned the gesture. "You have a blessed day as well. Good luck and tell Sherri that I forgive her and wish her the best. Tell her that I make sure that our two daughters are always in good hands, and that I visit them often at her mom's house. Also tell her that I make sure they don't go without the love of their father."

Jay smiled; "I will, thanks again. Goodbye." Then Jay walked toward the door while Sonny wheeled his chair behind him. "Goodbye," he said as the door closed.

Jay was so excited about the information he had just received that he ran to his car and drove straight to Gloria's house to let her hear the tape. After she listened to the tape, she became very hopeful. Then Jay went back to his office to get a search party together to locate the dead body.

CHAPTER TWENTY-FOUR

It's the next morning. Jay has called one of his friends, Don Beckman, a detective who conducts Grid searches for dead bodies or missing bones. Don is the supervisor in charge of the operation. The workers of the Grid search party team have gathered at an empty lot behind the city park. Everyone puts their heads together to decide a strategy that will help them locate the buried bones.

"Hey Don, how are you going to find this dead body, if there is one? Jay asked.

"Well to tell you the truth, since the crime was so long ago our search may be a little more difficult than I thought, however, it's been done before under more difficult circumstances. At least we have a direct target area to search. They'll dig in the area mentioned until they see something that may give them a clue. But don't worry, my guys have been doing this for years. They know what to look for and how to get the job done quickly. So, if there's a dead body around here, trust me, we'll find it!" Don said with confidence.

After hearing Don's explanation, Jay is impressed because he has never had to summons anyone to do this type of search.

"That sounds good to me." Jay said holding his chin and smiling. "Let me just step back and let you guys do your job." Due to the severe nature of the investigation, and the personal stake he had with the case, Jay's curiosity and the possible break in La Vonne's trial got the best of him. His interest caused him to stay around, where he went back to his car that was parked close by, and worked on some paperwork he had brought with him. Gloria was waiting at home for his call of any news.

A few hours had passed with no sighting of a dead body. Still curious, Jay kept a watch on what was going on from his car. After about four hours into the search, one of the search party workers yelled; "Hey Don, I think I found something over here!"

The yells of the worker magnified Jay's curiosity, causing him to quickly run to the scene as well; "What is it? What did you find?" He said with anticipation.

Don walked over to where Jay was standing and responded; "These are definitely human bones and also a few human teeth. Now we have to figure out if these are the bones you're looking for, or if they're someone else's bones. But they're definitely human bones and teeth." Jay smiled as he looked down at the pieces of dried up bones and teeth in the dirt.

The thought and reality of what Jay was seeing made him frown, feeling a little sick. "Alright, I've seen enough for one day. I'm going back to my office now. I need to find out the identity of the person killed so we can place a name with his identification. Then I'll try to get his dental records. So, if anything else comes up, call me on my cell or at the office." Jay said to Don as he prepared to leave the digging site.

Don smiled, knowing that the sight of human bones was hard for a lot of people to handle who weren't used to it. "Alright, I'll be in touch. I'm surprised you lasted this long." Don said and laughed.

"Very funny." Jay said and laughed back and continued; "I'll see ya!" Then he walked back to his car.

"Bye." Don responded.

After reaching his car, Jay took off and called Gloria to give her the news. He also called Sonny and asked him for the name of the dead guy.

After reaching his office, Jay made several calls. The time had passed very fast, it was becoming late. During the process of making the calls, Jay had obtained the name of the dead man from Sonny. It was Ryan Dennison. He had also received a faxed copy of Ryan's police report. Jay was still waiting to hear about any documented information regarding a dentist Ryan may have visited before he died.

The dental records would insure a positive identification for the search team and investigators on the bones found. Due to the lateness of the hour, Jay decided to leave the task of receiving the dental records for his secretary to handle first thing the next morning so that he could go home and get some much needed rest.

CHAPTER TWENTY-FIVE

It's early in the morning at Gloria's house. Eighteen year old Jr. and sixteen year old Stacy are in high school. They both have raging teenaged hormones, especially Stacy. Jr. now stands six feet two, weighing 185 pounds. He has many girls interested in him, but no special girlfriend right now. He's a very respectful young man. Stacy is five feet five. She weights 150 pounds and has all the right curves on her body, attracting many boys, including the most popular one at school, Teddy. Besides having a body to die for, many girls also envy her because she's nice, cute and has naturally long curly black hair.

Jr. and Stacy are getting ready to leave for school. "Grandma, can I go to Taco Bell with Teddy after school?" Stacy says.

Gloria looked at her with an unsure look; "Stacy, I don't really like that boy for you. He doesn't treat you right. You're a smart and pretty girl. You need to find someone who'll treasure you, and treat you like you deserve to be treated, with respect. Anytime a boy constantly makes excuses about meeting your family is not good news. That young man needs to learn how to respect adults. I just don't have a good feeling about him. So you come straight home after school, you hear me young lady?" She said with an authoritative tone.

Stacy frowned, feeling like she was being treated like a child. "But Grandma, I'm 16 years old now and you're still treating me like a child. I love Teddy. He's our school's quarterback. Any girl would be happy to be with him, but he wants to be with me."

Gloria knew that she needed to remind Stacy who was in charged. She did not want to lose control with her teenage

Momma, Please Forgive Me!

grandchildren. "I'll tell you what young lady. If this Teddy guy wants to have anything to do with you, he's gonna have to come through me first!" Gloria said with her hands on her hips. "Because if you let him get away with treating you any ole' way in the beginning, you'll never gain his respect. Stacy, in order to be treated like a lady, you have to act like one first! Do you understand young lady?"

Stacy looked at her grandmother and pouted; "Ahhh Grandma, you're just old fashioned. And if I keep telling him I can't do things with him he's gonna find somebody else to be with."

"Good!" Gloria responded as she continued; "Then let him go. Because if a young man can't respect the rules set by a young lady's family, then he doesn't need to be around her at all! So that's it! You come straight home after school. End of conversation!" Then Gloria continued cleaning the dishes left after breakfast.

After Gloria spoke, Stacy became mad, rolling her eyes at Gloria while her back was turned. Then she became bold; "I'm never going to have a boyfriend the way you treat me! I'm going to end up an ole' maid, just like you!" Stacy said with a very sassy tone.

Suddenly, all Stacy saw were stars! Gloria had stopped cleaning, turned around and slapped her right in the mouth, making her fall to the ground. Stacy was so stunned by Gloria's reaction that she looked at her grandmother like she had lost her mind. The slap was so hard that Stacy's light-skinned face turned bright red, leaving Gloria's hand-print on her cheek. The sting of the slap caused Stacy to cry while she held her face in her hand. "Why did you hit me?"

Gloria was furious! She looked Stacy dead in her eye and pointed her finger directly in her face; "Girl let me tell you one damn thing! Forgive me Lord for swearing." looking up to God for forgiveness and continued; "As long as you're living under my roof, don't ever sass me like that again! If you do, child, I swear I'll knock you silly. Stacy, don't you ever disrespect me like that again, especially in my own house! And after all I've done for you child, oh no! And if you do, you'll be finding a new place to live! And when I put you out, I want to see if that Teddy boy will take care of you. I want to see just how much he loves you then. Now, go to school. And you better be home on time or I'm coming after you, and you ain't gonna like that. Do you hear me young lady?"

Stacy shakes her head in agreement with Gloria while sniffing and wiping her eyes. She knew that she had definitely pushed the wrong button. Gloria is looking at her with fury in her eyes, daring her to try it again. "Yes Grandma. I'm sorry. I didn't mean to get smart with you. I'm sorry." Stacy slowly gets up from the floor and moves away from Gloria's reach.

After she stands up Gloria hugs her. "Stacy you have to understand that I only want the best for you. I don't want you to get caught up in a situation like your mother did. I want you to have high values and goals for yourself. I also want you to know that if a man is disrespecting you, you don't have to put up with it. If you don't gain his respect in the beginning, you'll never earn his respect at the end. So, child always know that Grandma loves you and only wants the best for you. So, go to school and know that I love you!" Then she kisses Stacy on the forehead.

"I love you too Grandma, bye." Stacy is still wiping away the tears, while trying to fix her hair.

"Jr. hurry up so you won't be late." Gloria yells back to him.

Knowing what just happened to Stacy, Jr. wastes no time getting out the house. "I'm coming Grandma."

Stacy gathers her belongings and attempts to run out the door; "Bye Grandma, I love you, and I'll be right home after school."

Momma, Please Forgive Me!

"Stacy, don't you run out this house without giving me a hug. And you better come straight home, or I'll get you even better the next time. You kids aren't going to send me to an early grave. Now, give me a hug goodbye." Jr. and Stacy stop long enough to give Gloria a hug and run out the door. "Bye Grandma, I love you."

"I love you to. Bye." Then Gloria watches them run out the door and off to school. She takes a moment to sit down because she is out of breath and sweating. She begins thinking and praying about her future in raising her grandchildren. "Lord please give me strength. I'm too old to be raising teenagers. Please let their mother come home so she can deal with their teenage hormones and not me." Then she rocks in her chair and falls to sleep.

CHAPTER TWENTY-SIX

It's mid-afternoon at the research laboratory where the remains of the bones are being kept and reviewed. Jay enters the laboratory where Don is watching the team of specialists examine the bones.

"Hey Jay." Don says. "That was a real winner we found yesterday. Unfortunately the bones were so badly decomposed that we weren't able to make out the sex, or retrieve the entire body. It looks like an animal may have attacked the raw meat after it was placed in the hollow grave. Then it mutilated the evidence of the dead body way before anyone ever knew a crime had taken place. That's probably why no one found it sooner."

Jay frowned at the news. "Since I'm basing my entire case for an appeal on this evidence, will the incomplete findings jeopardize my case if this is Ryan Dennison?" he asked with curiosity.

"No it doesn't if you can find his dental records, because

we located a jaw with a complete set of teeth." Don said with an ounce of hope in his voice.

Jay was happy to get any ounce he could get. "Good, then give this to the examiners. I stopped by the prison and got a copy of the dental records before I came over here. I thought they might come in handy."

Don looks at the file, smiling. "Good work. Man you sure go the extra mile for your clients don't you!"

Jay's confident ego began to shine; "What can I say!" Joking around before getting serious. "But I'll tell you what, you don't build a good reputation by doing half-ass work, now do you?" Don shook his head no, while Jay continued; "So, when will we be able to get the results back? I got a client that wants to get out of prison. And with this new evidence, I should be able to get a quick appeal. Especially since there's another major fault on the part of the police department, by not responding to her calls!" They both looked at each other with a smirk on their face and shook their heads in disbelief.

"Man I gotta give it to you. If I'm ever killed, you're definitely the man I want to represent me and I'll put that information in my will. Because if these dental records match, and from what you've told me about the police never filing a report when Mr. Waters reported it, your client is as good as out of there!"

Don and Jay smile. They were both feeling more hopeful than ever. "So, when will we find something out?" Jay asked again.

"They should be able to give you more details tomorrow. So go home, or back to your office and start preparing for your opening arguments." Don said with confidence.

"Is that just a nice way to get rid of me?" Jay joked.

Don laughed; "If that's how you want to take it." Then he got serious. "But no, there's nothing else we can do here. I'm only the grid man, so we've done all we can do. The rest is up to the experts. So go on home and I'll call you as soon as I hear something."

"Alright. I'm out of here. See ya!" Then Jay gathered the rest of his belongings, put them in his briefcase and got ready to leave.

"See you tomorrow." Don said as he walked to another part of the research room with the dental file in hand. Jay walked to his car and drove to the prison to fill La Vonne in on the possible good news.

****

The afternoon has become late. Jay is waiting for La Vonne to come to the meeting room where he's waiting. When she walks in, she begins to blush. "Hi Jay, what brings you here?" she says with curiosity while thinking; "I hope it's to see more of me than you ever have before, because I can sure make good use out of a good man like you!"

Jay was innocent to La Vonne's thoughts and continued with his news that had him feeling positive and energetic. "Hopefully good news."

La Vonne begins to feel positive and energetic from his response, yet, unsure. "'Hopefully' good news? What exactly does that mean?"

"It's not for sure, but things are looking very good for your case. The information you got from Sherri was a very big help. In fact, because of Sherri you just might get out of here sooner than later."

La Vonne looked at him with a puzzled look of excitement on her face. "For real? For real? Don't be pulling my leg Jay. I might get out of this place soon?"

Jay was enjoying La Vonne's excitement. "You know me

better than that, I only deal with the truth. Your case is much too serious for me to play around with. I thought a little good news would help you hang in there a little longer, because if it's in God's plan, you'll be out of here real soon."

La Vonne jumped up and down with pure excitement; "Yes! Yes!!! I've been waiting to hear something close to those words for ten long years. But once I hear the words 'I'm free,' that'll be all I need to hear for the rest of my life! So, when will we find out something? Anything?"

Jay laughed; "Calm down, calm down. Don't get too excited yet. Everything is not confirmed. But things do look good and totally in your favor."

La Vonne held her arms up high, praying; "Thank you Lord! Thank you! I knew you'd get me out of this place." Then she looked at Jay and hugged him, then backed down from the gracious hug after noticing his uneasiness; "So, what's next?"

Due to her hug, Jay flinched. He did not want La Vonne to get the wrong impression of him, or the results to his news. "Well, we wait for the results of a test I requested. I should get them by tomorrow. So lady, hang in there, and when you get out, dinner is on me!" Jay wasn't sure if he should even offer, because he didn't want La Vonne to expect something that he did not have in mind.

La Vonne was all smiles. "Now you're making me want to break out just to hold you to that date."

Jay laughed. "I wouldn't do that if I were you. Besides, your day will come soon enough. So, just hang in there a little longer. I gotta go now. I just wanted to personally give you a little good news to carry you through."

"That kind of news will surely hold me over, thanks!" La Vonne again hugged Jay, again leaving him feeling uneasy.

"You're welcomed. Oh yeah, tell Sherri that I said thanks for the information, and let her know that Sonny forgives her. Also

Momma, Please Forgive Me!

tell her that he's a minister now. So thanks to her, and especially Sonny, you should be walking out of here real soon. So, take care and I'll be in touch."

"I'm holding you to your words. Bye."

"No matter what, I won't let you down La Vonne. Goodbye." Then he left the building. La Vonne smiled all the way back to her cell, feeling like she was floating on cloud nine.

CHAPTER TWENTY-SEVEN

It's after ten in the evening at Gloria's house. The children have just turned off the lights to go to bed. Suddenly, the phone rings. Stacy jumps out bed and runs; "I'll get it," she yells.

Gloria is unsettled by the late caller, nevertheless, she doesn't become alarmed because she knows, and her grandchildren know that they can not accept calls after nine. Therefore, she's curious as to why Stacy is so quick to answer the phone. "Who is it Stacy?" Gloria said with interest and concern.

After realizing who the caller is, Stacy blushes; "It's for me Grandma. A friend from school." she yells out.

"I hope you're not planning on taking that call at this late hour." Gloria reminds her.

"I'm getting off Grandma. I just have to tell my friend something real quick." Gloria continues mending a few clothes. Stacy returns to the caller and quickly takes the phone back to her bedroom and closes the door so no one can hear her conversation.

Gloria notices Stacy's actions, but is not sure if she should enforce her strict rules, or wait and see if Stacy will do the right thing while she continues sewing.

Stacy addresses the caller; "Hi, I'm back," she says with a sweet voice.

"Hey sweet thang. What happened to you after school? I was looking for you." Stacy's boyfriend Teddy said.

"I had to come straight home. I told Kelly to tell you I had to leave."

Teddy became furious with her answer; "Kelly? You're supposed to talk to me yourself. Don't send someone else to talk for you. You're supposed to be my lady, aren't you, not Kelly!" Stacy replies with embarrassment. "I am your girlfriend."

Teddy's attitude was very demanding and forceful. "Well why couldn't you tell me yourself? Did your Grandma tell you to come straight home again?" he said sarcastically.
"Yes." she said with fear and intimidation.

"Besides, why do you live with your grandmother in the first place? Where's your mother?"

Stacy did not want Teddy to know that her mother was in prison. She thought that if any of her friends knew what really happened to her mother, she would become the laugh of the school. It had been so long since La Vonne had been locked up, so no one in the family made it a known fact where she actually was. So, when asked about her mothers location, the questioned was answered; "I don't know. I haven't seen her in years. She left a long time ago and my grandmother has taken care of me and my brother every since she left."

"Well, where ever your mother is, you still need to learn that you're not a child and start standing up to your Grandma? You're old enough to do what you want to do. Hell, if my parents told me to come straight home after school, I'd tell them to go to hell. You see I'm a man now and they ain't got shit to tell me. I'm also the most popular brother on campus, and the star of the football team. So, if I can't spend time with my lady when I want to, I'll find someone I can spend time with. Besides, I can't have a girlfriend who can't speak up for herself. All that baby shit

Momma, Please Forgive Me!

should have stayed behind when you left middle school. So, what's it gonna be like?"

Stacy became fearful and nervous. Teddy's demands were scaring her. She had seen him mad before and didn't want him to become mad at her. "I can speak up for myself. It's just that my Grandmother had something else for me to do, that's all. When do you think you can come over to meet her? She's been asking to meet you for a while."

"Don't you know by now. I don't need no grown folks in my damn business. I don't get in theirs, so why they want to get in mine? Now, either you gonna be with me, or you're not!" he continued with his forceful tone. Then his tone quickly changed, only to put a guilt trip on her; "So tell me pretty girl, what's it gonna be?"

Stacy blushed at his tone. "I'll meet you after school tomorrow. Is that alright?"

"I got better plans than meeting after school. Why don't you come over my house before you go to school. My parents will be at work and we'll be all alone. That way we can spend some quality time together before I go to football practice, if you know what I mean."

Knowing exactly what he was talking about, his words frightened Stacy, causing her to become nervous again, but not wanting him to know how she really felt, she replied; "I know what you mean."

"Well, what's it gonna be? Either tomorrow or not at all. I can't have my lady standing me up and not giving me a little sumthin', sumthin'. So, you either gonna be with me or you're not."

Stacy tried to keep her voice to a whisper so her grandmother wouldn't remember that she was still on the phone. "I'll be there."

Knowing that he was getting his way, Teddy smiled with

confidence. "That's more like it. Now, I gotta get off this phone and take care of some business. I'll see you in the morning, and don't keep me waiting."

"I won't. I'll be there. Bye."

"Later," he said.

Stacy felt sick, knowing what Teddy expected her virgin body to do.

Suddenly Gloria comes into Stacy's room as she's laying on her bed thinking about Teddy. "Stacy, who was that on the phone?"

Stacy is frighted by Gloria's unexpected visit and gives her a quick answer; "It was my friend Kim."

"Kim? I don't think I've heard you talk much about Kim. Who is she?"

Suddenly Stacy became nervous, knowing she was lying, remembering back to this morning when Gloria slapped her to the floor. "She's a new girl. She hasn't been at our school very long. She doesn't have many friends and wanted to know if I would walk to school with her tomorrow. Her house is on the way." Stacy is crossing her figures behind her back, hoping her story is acceptable. "Alright, but don't be late."

Stacy is happy with Gloria's response; "We won't. Goodnight Grandma."

Gloria bends down to hug Stacy. "Goodnight and I love you very much."

"I love you too Grandma." Stacy says while she gets back under her covers to go to sleep. Gloria picks up the telephone and walks out of Stacy's room and closes the door.

"Jr., are you in bed yet?" Gloria yells.

"Yes Grandma."

Gloria opens his cracked door, peaks in and smiles; "Well get up and give me a hug. You know I want a hug before you go to bed. I don't care how old you get. As long as you're in my house I always want my goodbye and goodnight hugs."

Jr. hugged Gloria and got into his bed. Gloria turned off all the lights, turned off her sewing machine and also got into her bed. The house became quiet as everyone went to sleep.

CHAPTER TWENTY-EIGHT

It's eight o'clock the next morning. Stacy has arrived at Teddy's front door when she should be at school. She knocks and Teddy immediately opens the door, greeting her with a big smile; "Hey beautiful."

She's nervous and quickly walks inside before anyone recognizes her. "Hey yourself," she says with a big smile.

After walking in, Teddy closes the front door and they immediately begin kissing, all the way to his bedroom. Stacy peaks with one eye opened and one closed, nervous as to what's about to happen and where they're heading. After reaching his room, he quickly closes the door behind them. "I missed you," he says while attempting to warm her up to his motives.

"I missed you too." she says with a little confidence as she looks around his room. "Your house is nice. I've never seen the inside."

While still embrassed, Teddy swings her back and forth. "Well, we're going to have to change all that aren't we? So, lets get down to business. We don't have a lot of time." he says while taking his hand and stroking it across her shoulders, pushing her shirt off her arm. Her nervousness grows, knowing that having sex is something she has never done before.

Teddy wastes no time in having things go his way. "I'll be right back," he smiles and says as he leaves the room, leaving her alone. While he's gone, Stacy begins to nervously look around the room that's filled with football memorabilia. The room is also filled with newspaper clippings and photos of Teddy at football games. She knows that what she's about to do will be her first time. She also knows that she's disobeying her Grandmother, which she doesn't feel good about. Teddy appears again, wearing nothing but a condom and a smile.

"So pretty lady. Are you ready for me? As you can see, I've been ready for you!" he said smiling with confidence.

Stacy's eyes grow larger than saucers. She had never seen a naked man standing right before her like this before, especially one who's private part was standing straight and tall, saluting her with pride. She didn't know if she should run as fast as she could, escaping his desires, or stay and be the woman he expected her to be, even though she knew she was going against her own feelings. What she did know was if she ran, she would be the laugh of the entire school. She also knew that she would lose the boy she thought she loved. She did not want either to happen, so she tried to be strong and answered; "Uhh, ready? Well, you know it's my first time, so you'll have to be gentle with me," she said with hesitation.

"Gentle? Well, from what I've heard, being gentle is my middle name. So, lay down and relax, and let me be nice and gentle with you." Having sex was not new to Teddy. In fact, having sex was something he expected all of his girlfriends to do with him, or he didn't give them the time of his day.

So, while he attempted to convince her to relax, Stacy closed her eyes and braced herself for what was to come. He began kissing her around her neck while undressing her at the same time. Stacy peeked out of one eye, afraid of what was to come. Then he laid her on the bed and caressed her naked body. She laid there shaking, trying to be a woman, while her thoughts reminded her that she was only a little girl.

Teddy could feel her body trembling. "What's the matter baby? Don't be scared. I promise I'll be gentle!" Then he continued kissing her while trying to make love to his virgin girlfriend. Making love to virgins was something he made a habit of doing.

While he attempted to make love to Stacy, she squirmed from the pain she was feeling from his penetration. "How does it feel?" he asked.

"It's fine," she said with fear, trying to not show her pain as he continued.

"Ahh, you feel so good! Yeah, you feel real good!" he moaned with his eyes closed, still wearing a smile as he moved up and down on her naked body.

As she laid there in great pain, she thought about the actions that were taking place, knowing she wasn't ready for what she was doing. While she laid there in silence, a few tears came from her eyes, as the experience grew more painful. However, she refused to voice her pain and feelings.

Laying there exposing her naked body to a boy for the very first time, along with releasing her virginity to someone she felt she loved was nothing short of frightening. However, knowing that she could lose Teddy if she didn't give him what he wanted stayed on her mind, causing her to continue laying in silence, attempting to enjoy the experience. "This is not what I wanted to do with him," she thought while he continued to ride up and down on her body like she was an animal, making sounds and comments she had never heard. "Yeah baby! Umm, umm, umm this shit is good!"

As she laid still, making faces of fear and pain, Teddy never noticed, because he was submerged in the enjoyment of the voyage he was exploring. The more he rode, the more her mind wondered; "I've only been going out with him for two weeks.

How can I stop him? But if I do, that'll be the end of our relationship, and he's the most popular and cutest guy in school. Every girl in school would love to be with him, but he picked me. Oh well, I better try to enjoy this sex thing if I'm going to be with him. Besides, who ever said that having sex was so great anyway? All I know is that it hurts."

"Ouch!" Stacy quietly said as the ride got rougher. "Are you alright?" he said with concern.

"I'm fine. It was just hurting a little, but I'm fine," she said while convincing him that things were alright. Then she continued to lay in total stillness, enduring the uncontrollable pain, trying to take it like she was an experienced woman.

Suddenly, Teddy came up for a little air and offered a few words of what he considered comfort. "So, how does it feel baby?" he said while continuing his voyage with sweat running down his chest, onto hers. "Am I being gentle with you?"

Stacy tried to remain brave. "It feels good," she uttered with a frown on her face. While he continued, he avoided her true feelings, constantly keeping his eyes closed, still wearing a big smile of satisfaction.

Suddenly, to her surprise it was over. Due to the soreness of her once virgin body, she hoped he was finished and wasn't just taking a break, because her fragile body couldn't take much more. While still wearing a frown, she tried to act like she enjoyed the entire experience. Then, when he raised off her drenched body and put his clothes on, she was relieved that it was finally over. Her painful encounter assured her of not looking forward to another sexual experience with anyone any time soon. Suddenly, she began to worry about how she would get out of the next time around. However, the only thing on her mind right now was that they were through.

"So baby, when can we get together again? Because,

Momma, Please Forgive Me!

being with you was something else!" Teddy said with great confidence, thinking he'd rocked her world.

Stacy quickly put on her clothes and noticed a little blood on the sheet where she laid. Seeing the blood frightened her, causing her to worry without exposing her true feelings, making her respond hesitantly; "I'm not sure. You know I can't miss too much school. Because if my grandmother finds out, she'll be mad." As she moved, she was reminded by the unforgettable pain and the sight of her own blood of what she had just done.

Suddenly, Teddy's good mood changed, causing him to speak with force; "Look, I told you that I'm your man! You're gonna have to work things out with your grandmother, or it won't work with us."

Due to his harsh tone, Stacy jumped and became afraid. "I will. I promise I will."

Then he smiled, knowing he was again getting his way. "That's more like it. Now, let me finish getting dressed so we can get back to school. I'll be in big trouble if I'm late for football practice." Then they went back to school, with Stacy barely saying a word while Teddy smiled the entire way back.

CHAPTER TWENTY-NINE

It's mid afternoon at Jay's office. His secretary has answered the telephone and buzzes him to take the call. "Hello, this is Jay."

"Hey Jay, this is Don. I got really good news for you buddy." he says with excitement.

"I'm ready."

"It's a match! The dental records confirm that the bones we found are in fact Ryan Dennison's. I also found out that his family filed a missing persons report on him years ago."

Jay is happy, but confused; "They did? Hmm. I'll have to check into that. That might add to our case," he said, while scheming up another angle that would help La Vonne's case.

"Good job counselor! So, file that appeal and get that young lady out of prison. Also, do you want to contact that young man's family or should I?"

"I'll take care of that. Besides, I may need one of them to testify in court. Maybe they can piece the entire story together for us, which would be an added benefit to our case."

"Well go for it." Don was pleased with how things were turning out. He knew that their work was a strong and positive force that could help in La Vonne's defense.

"Don, you never let me down. I can always count on you. Thanks man. I'll be in touch."

"Hopefully on better terms." Don said.

"I hope so too. I'll go to the lab later and pick up those results. Take care and thanks again, and have a good day. Bye."
"You do the same, and glad I could help."

After ending his call, Jay got on the telephone and immediately called Gloria to tell her the good news.
"Hello." Gloria said.

"Hello, Miss Johnson. This is Jay. I have some good news about La Vonne's case.

Gloria beamed with joy; "You do? Thank God! Oh thank God! What did you find out? Tell me!" she said with excitement.

"Calm down so I can tell you." he laughed and continued; "The bones are a match with Ryan Dennison's DNA. Now I need to follow up on a few other leads. Then I should be able to present my case to get La Vonne another appeal."

"That's music to my ears. Jay, you have definitely been a God send to our family. I thank God for you every night, and I

Momma, Please Forgive Me!

thank God for all the help you've given us."

"Thank you Miss Johnson. Your words are very kind. I just wanted to tell you the good news. So, I'll be in touch when I find any other news."

"I'll be waiting for your call."

"Ok, take care and I'll be in touch. Goodbye." After their call, Jay left his office and went to his car so he could meet with Ryan Dennison's family.

Gloria hung up her phone. She was so happy that she danced in the spirit of God, giving thanks to God, holding her hands up high.

****

The day has now passed into the afternoon. Jay has arrived at the home of Ryan Dennison. The house is a modern styled home. The neighborhood is well-kept and quiet. Jay approaches the front door and rings the bell, waiting for someone to answer.

A middle-aged light-skinned African-American lady opens the door and is curious as to who's at her front door. "Can I help you?" she says as she looks through the webbed metal bars door.

Jay can not clearly see her face, but answers; "Yes you can. I'm looking for the family members of Ryan Dennison."

Astonished by his request, she answered curiously; "I'm his mother. Ryan's not here. Can I help you?"

Jay slides his business card through the metal door for a proper introduction. "Hello Mrs. Dennison. My name is Bethel Jay Mitchell. I'm an attorney who is representing a client who was indirectly connected with your son."

Mrs. Dennison is still confused as to what Jay wants and

why he's at her front door. Her attitude is calm, but curious and concerned; "How is your client connected to my son? I haven't seen or heard from him in over eleven years. Have you found him?" she says with great hope.

"I'm afraid I have. May I come in and talk to you privately?" Jay responds with sorrow.

Still unsure but curious, Mrs. Dennison lets him enter her home. "Sure, come on in. This is my husband." Mr. Dennison stands from his reclining chair and shakes Jay's hand. Jay gives him a business card. "Have a seat Mr. Mitchell."

Jay returns the gesture and sits down on the couch. "Hello Mr. Dennison, my name is attorney Bethel Jay Mitchell."

"What can we do for you Mr. Mitchell?" Mr. Dennison says firmly.

"First of all I'd like to tape our conversation. I may need to use your statement in court. Is that alright with both of you?"

Mrs. Dennison looks at her husband, then at Jay with a very confused look on her face. Then they both respond; "Sure, just tell us what information you have on our son?"

Jay didn't know exactly how to tell them the truth, so he stalled, trying to soften the news. "Well, I have some good news and some bad news."

Mrs. Dennison was unsure as to what he meant, causing her to become frightened by his expressions. "What's the good news?" hoping it would soften the bad news.
"Your son has been found."

Not wanting to become too excited, Mr. Dennison braced himself for the bad news. "And the bad news?"
"He was killed over eleven years ago."

Suddenly Mrs. Dennison cried; "Oh my God. I knew he was dead. I just knew he was dead. It was those thugs who did it, wasn't it?"

Mr. Dennison was trying to remain strong through his pain and concern. "Do you know who did it?"

"We think so. But we're not one hundred percent sure yet. Do either of you have any idea as to who may have killed your son?"

Mrs. Dennison responded with a great deal of grief in her voice, while still crying from the news. "We heard stories about him possibly being killed by some thugs. But no one ever found his body. Where did you find it?"

"My client is in prison for killing her abusive husband. We think that it was her husband who killed your son. We found him in a hallow grave next to the park where the man lived. It's not too far from your home."

Listening to the news saddened Mrs. Dennison, causing her to hysterically cry for the lost of her son and where he was found. "Oh my God. Those bastard's! Please forgive me Lord. But how could someone do such a thing? He was a human being. Why? Why?' she constantly repeated while her husband rocked her in his arms.

Mr. Dennison was trying to console his wife, even though he knew the news was hard on him as well. "I can't believe this. I just can't believe that someone would be so vicious as to do something like that to another human being. Now, what do we do?"

Jay felt really sad for the Dennison's as he observed their painful reactions. However, he knew that he needed to tell them the bad news in order to get down to the bottom of what was going on. He also knew that he needed to get any information he could in order to free La Vonne. As they held each other tight and cried, Jay tried to soften the harsh blow they had just been given. He tried to help them somehow see the bright side of this very dark picture. "Well, you can have a funeral if you'd like. By giving Ryan a proper funeral service may give you some closure with his death. I can only imagine that the waiting and wondering of his fate has been hard on everyone who knew and loved him."

Mrs. Dennison found a little comfort in Jay's words. "Yes! Yes! That's what we'll do. We never got a chance to give him an official farewell. We kept hoping that one day he'd walk through the door and tell us that everything was alright, but he never did, which kept us wondering for years. We knew that he was hanging out with a bad crowd who were doing drugs. But we always held on to a hope and prayer that someday he'd come home."

Jay smiled, knowing that even though he was delivering bad news, something good could now come out of the results. "Exactly. So, now do you understand why it's so important for me to know the entire story? By knowing the entire story I can free an abused woman, allowing her the opportunity of raising her children who love and miss her dearly. Then I can determine that her deceased husband is the same man who killed your son. Then your minds can be put to rest knowing that the killer is also dead and won't be able to hurt anyone else. So, can you tell me what part of the story you did hear?"

Mrs. Dennison looked at her husband with compassion in her eyes and responded; "We heard that a guy who was high on drugs killed him. I think his name was John or something like that." Jay suddenly became excited. "Was it Jonathan?" he hoped.

"That's it! I'm sure that's the name my daughter heard them say. But she also said she heard that somebody killed that guy. Is that true? Is he dead or just missing like our son was?" Mrs. Dennison said with fear and curiosity.

"No ma'am, he's dead. Like I said earlier, his wife, my client, killed him in self defense. She was an abused wife and did what she thought was right to protect herself and her children. I'm trying to get her released from prison right now. So, you said that your daughter found the information on your son's killer? Is she here? Can I talk to her?" Jay looked around the room for their

Momma, Please Forgive Me!

daughter.

"No she's not." Mrs. Dennison responded with a sad tone. "She lives out of town now. After Ryan disappeared she discovered some information on his killer. After that, her life was threatened, so she moved out of state. We heard that the guy who killed him was a part of a heavy drug ring that had a lot of power in the community. The word was out that if anyone spoke a word about what happened to Ryan, they too would be dead. After waking up one morning and finding a dead black cat on our doorstep with a note saying, you'll be next, we couldn't take any chances. So we packed her clothes, she quit her job and left town that very same day."

"Is there anyway I can talk to her? Anyway at all?" he said with hope.

Mrs. Dennison looked at her husband, they had an emptiness and uncertain look on their face. Then, they looked at Jay and she responded; "I don't see why not. Especially if it'll help your client become free, along with helping the memory of my son rest in peace. Let me get her telephone number for you. Just tell her who you are, what you're doing and that I told you to call. But don't give her number to anyone else. This number is very private. Even though it has been over eleven years, we still don't want anyone to locate her. After that experience, she's still afraid to even come home and visit. So, now that we know Ryan's killer is dead, maybe she can come back home." Then she went to her telephone book and got Jay the telephone number. "Here you are. Her name is Jenny. Don't forget to tell her me and her dad said it was alright to talk to you."

Jay was very excited for the lead. "Thank you very much! This will help our case a lot. And don't worry, I won't give this number to anyone. You and your husband have been a very big help. You have my card, so if there's anything else I can do, just call. Also, here's the telephone number to the department that has your son's remains. Call them and they will tell you what you need to do to get your son's remains to a funeral home of your choice." Then Jay gathered his belongings to prepare to leave.

Mr. and Mrs. Dennison stood up and shook Jay's hand while smiling. "Thank you. We miss our son, but the crowd he was hanging with and the drugs he was taking, we just knew that something awful was bound to happen. We tried our best to get him away from them, but he was a grown man. He wouldn't listen to us. Thank you again Mr. Mitchell for your help. Now, we can at least give our son a final farewell."

"You're very welcomed. And I'm sorry to be the one to pass on the bad news. Both of you have a good evening. You know how to reach me if needed. Good evening."

They both responded; "You too, and Thank you again. Good evening," as they walked him to the door. Jay got in his car and drove to the lab to get the results of the dead body.

CHAPTER THIRTY

It's late in the afternoon at Gloria's house. She's in the kitchen cooking dinner when Jr. walks into the room. "Grandma, what's for dinner? I'm hungry."

"Child, you're always hungry." she jokingly said. "I guess that's why you've grown so tall. Aren't you six foot tall by now?" "Six-one." he says as he grabs some cookies out of the jar.

"And with all that you eat, you're still as skinny as a string bean. Well, I'm fixing some fried chicken, macaroni and cheese, green beans and hot-water corn bread. How does that sound?" Gloria smiled while watching the excited expression on Jr.'s face as she told him what they were going to eat.

Momma, Please Forgive Me!

"That sounds real good Grandma. I really can't wait to eat now." He said as cookie crumbs dropped from his face.

"Well, dinner will be ready in about an hour. So have a small snack, and not anymore cookies, if you're that hungry." he stopped short of reaching for another cookie and opend the refrigerator, sticking his head deep inside to look for another snack. Then Gloria continued; "Where's your sister? Didn't she walk home with you? It's getting late." Gloria was beginning to worry.

"Grandma, I'm a senior now. I can't be seen walking home with Stacy. But I did see her walking with one of her friends. She should be here shortly."

Jr. left the kitchen snacking on some cheese and crackers while Gloria continued cooking. Her thoughts grew stronger about Stacy. "She better be here shortly, or her butt is mine! And I mean that." While Gloria's thoughts about Stacy grew more intense, her stirring of the macaroni and cheese grew strong, causing a few noodles to pop out of the pot. "I just don't know what I'm going to do with that girl. At least I don't have to worry about Jr. getting pregnant. These kids, Lord help me! I sure hope I have enough strength to keep up with them and their teenaged hormones."

Shortly after, Gloria emerged from her thoughts as Stacy walked into the house. "Hi Grandma, I'm home." she says with a big smile on her face.

"How was school baby?" Gloria said smiling, trying to not act concerned of her delay. She was still stirring her macaroni and cheese with great force.

Stacy becomes fearful by Gloria's question, the look in her eye and her suspicious tone. "School? Why do you ask Grandma?" She fears that Gloria found out she went over Teddy's house before school and lost her virginity.

Gloria's eyes meets Stacy's head-on. She wonders why she panicked to her question. "I always ask you about your school day.

Why are you so defensive? Did something go on today that I should know about?" Gloria says while looking above her glasses that were resting on her chubby and sweaty cheeks.

Stacy becomes nervous, knowing that she would be in big trouble if Gloria discovered the truth. She stutters; "Noooo ma'ammmm, everything was fine today at school. But I gotta go do my homework now. Call me when dinner's ready, bye." Then she quickly ran to her bedroom to get away from Gloria's suspicious questions.

After Stacy left the room, Gloria thought about Stacy's strange behavior and wondered what was really going on. "Hmm, that girl sure is acting strange today. I bet it's got something to do with that so-called boyfriend of hers. I wish she would just convince him to come over so I can meet him. I don't like it when I don't know what's going on in her life and who she's hanging around with. It doesn't take much to get with the wrong crowd these days. That's something I sure don't want is for her to be hanging in the wrong crowd. I know that being in high school can add a lot of peer pressure to any child. I just worry about her because she always stays to herself. I'll have to start keeping a closer eye on her. I need to make sure she's not getting involved in anything she has no business getting involved in. It just seems that girls are always affected by images, and what their friends think, far more than boys do. Thank God Jr.'s friends are all nice and respectable young men who come around the house all the time. With him, I don't have to worry about anything, other than his short temper. But with her, God please give me strength." Then Gloria continued preparing her food. "Jr., are you alright?" She yelled out.

After hearing the earlier conversation between Gloria and Stacy, Jr. was also becoming concerned by Gloria's suspicious questions. As he walked in the room with Gloria, he was hoping that

Momma, Please Forgive Me!

she wasn't setting them up for something she knew about and they didn't know she knew. "Yes Grandma, I'm fine, why?"

"I heard you talking in your sleep last night. Child, are you sure you're alright? Are you still having those nightmares?"

Jr. was depressed, realizing what his grandmother's concerns involved. "Yes Grandma. I'm still having them. Sometimes I'm alright, then other times, I can't seem to block them out. But I'll get over it someday. You don't have to worry about me. I'll be fine."

Gloria became very concerned with his response. "Well maybe you need to go talk to Pastor George again. The dreams seemed to stop when you were seeing him awhile ago. What do you think? Do you want me to make an appointment for you?"

"No thank you grandma, I'll be alright. I think this is just something I'll have to get over. Really, I'll be alright." He tried to assure her that he could handle things like a man.

However, she wasn't so sure that was possible. "Are you sure?"

"Yes, Grandma, I'm sure. But thanks for asking. I love you." Then he hugged and kissed her on the cheek.

"I love you to baby." Gloria said while returning his hug. She was trying to be understanding about his need to handle things himself. "Well, go finish your homework. I'll call you when dinner's ready."

"Ok."

Then she finished preparing her meal while the kids did their homework."

CHAPTER THIRTY-ONE

Two days have passed since Jay has talked to the Dennison

family and their daughter Jenny. He has gathered enough information from them for his case and has put in a request for La Vonne to have another appeal. It's late in the afternoon. Jay is in his office preparing for his next move when his secretary buzzes him regarding a call; "Jay, I have a Mr. Daniel Swanson on the telephone. He says he's from the Office of Appeals. Do you want to take the call?"

Jay became excited, yet anxious to hear what he had to say. "Yes please! Put him through. Thank you." Then he clicked over to the call and changed his excited tone to that of firm, but concerned; "Hello, this is Mr. Mitchell speaking. How can I help you Mr. Swanson?"

In a very firm and confident manner Mr. Swanson responded; "Good afternoon Mr. Mitchell. My name is Daniel Swanson. I'm from the Office of Appeals. We received your documents a few days ago requesting an appeal for your client, Ms. La Vonne Brown. Due to the nature of the evidence you submitted regarding her case, the courts have reserved an emergency date to meet with you and your client for an appeal hearing."

Jay was so happy to hear the news, yet remained calm; "Ok. So when is the date scheduled for?"

"Next week. A week from today at 9 AM." Daniel firmly responded.

Jay tried to keep a cool and professional demeanor. "Did you say a week from today?"

"Yes Sir, I did. The judge felt that this case was far to important to put off any longer. So, will that date work for you and your client?"

"Sure, it'll be just fine. We'll be there. Thank you very much."

"Good, then we'll expect you and your client at nine in the

morning a week from today. Have a nice day Mr. Mitchell."

"You too Mr. Daniels and thank you for your call." Suddenly Jay was listening to the dial tone, speechless and excited! He immediately called Gloria to tell her the good news.

"Hello." Gloria answers.

"Miss Johnson?"

"Jay? Is that you?" she said with curiosity.

"Yes it is, I'm sorry Miss Johnson. I was so excited that I forgot to tell you who I was when you first answered. How are you today?"

She became very suspicious to his call and wanted to get straight to the point. "What are you so excited about? Is there some good news on La Vonne's case?" Gloria was ready to hear any good news Jay had to offer.

He was so excited that he could barely contain his happiness. "We did it! We did it! I just received a call from the court of appeals office. We have a court date next Tuesday at 9AM!"

Gloria was so happy that she cried, prayed and danced in the room around the telephone wire. "Thank God!!!! Oh Thank you Jesus!"

"So, will you be ready next week at nine?"

"Oh heavens yes! Wild horses couldn't keep me away!" Gloria said while continuing her dance.

"Good. Well I gotta go take care of some business. I just wanted you to be the first one to hear the good news. I'll be in touch."

"Thank you very much! That sure was good news, bye."

"Bye."

Gloria continues to dance and calls the kids in the room to share in the victory. "Jr. Stacy, come in here right now! Hurry!" she yells.

After hearing the excited tone in Gloria's voice, they quickly come into the room to see what she was going on. "What is it Grandma? What's going on?" they both ask with a puzzled, but excited look on their faces.

"Your mom is getting out of prison! Your mom is getting out of prison!" Jr. and Stacy looked at each other, then at their Grandmother joined in with the excitement. "Yeah!!!! Yeah!!! Alright!!"

Stacy is happy, but confused. She's happy that her mother may come home, but unsure and confused as to what she'll tell her friends and boyfriend where her mother has been for all these years. However, she still wants to know more information so she can be prepared. "Grandma, who told you that?"

Jr. also has a happy but confused look on his face. Over the last few years that he has developed into a man, he isn't sure if he can live with his mother again, knowing that she killed their father, leaving him without a fatherly figure to raise him and give him manly values. He's learned to accept that what his father did was wrong, but as he got older, he had a hard time forgiving his mother, or accepting that everything was alright. It was alright to go see her in prison from time to time, even though the visits became painful and fewer as he got older. He wasn't sure if he could accept her back into his life to raise him and his sister like nothing had ever happened if she were to come home. Although, his confusion was kept hidden deep within. His confusion was also a part of why his dreams did not go away as he grew older. However, he did not want to say or do the wrong thing to upset his grandmother. He and Stacy loved and accepted Gloria as their mother, leaving the past hidden from the outside world, keeping it their families little secret. They knew how good Gloria had been to them when they needed her most. So, for the sake of keeping his grandmother happy, he also tried to enjoy the news.

Momma, Please Forgive Me!

"I just got a call from your mother's lawyer. He told me that we have a court date next Tuesday at nine in the morning. I just know that they're going to let her out of prison. I can feel it in my bones. Lord, I just know it! Hallelujah!" Then Gloria continued dancing around the room, as the kids smiled and made the best of the news.

CHAPTER THIRTY-TWO

It's the next morning. The kids are at school when Teddy sees Stacy. "Hey girl! What's going on with my sweet thang?" then he kisses her on the lips.

She smiles at his gesture, feeling special. "Hey yourself. Things are well. Hey, I'm gonna miss you next week, I have somewhere to go, so I won't be at school." she said with excitement.

"That's nice." he responds. "Did you say next week? When next week?"

"Tuesday. Why, what's going on next week?" Stacy is puzzled by his question.

"Why? Baby, me and you are what's going on next week. That's why. Remember, we're suppose to be hooking up to do the wild thang again! I'm sure you want more by now. It's almost been a week. I know you didn't forget about our weekly meeting, or forget how good it was, did you?"

"No, I didn't forget. But my grandmother is getting a special award from the church. It's a very special honor, and it will be a very happy day for her. I can't let her down by not going. But I'll only be gone for that one day. We can do the wild thang another day." she says while smiling and holding his hands. Stacy was too embarrassed to tell him the real reason why she wouldn't be there.

155

Suddenly Teddy becomes angry and he drops her hands. "Oh, so I see how things are gonna be. You gonna put me off for your Grandma?"

"Wouldn't you?" She says while looking at him with a very serious look in her eyes. She can't believe what he's suggesting.

Then, in an arrogant tone Teddy responds with anger. "Oh, so I see where you're coming from. Whenever your family calls, you just drop me like a hot potato and run. Well, if that's how it's gonna be, then maybe,"

She stops him in his tracks. "Don't say it! I do love you and I do want to be with you. But this is a very special day for my grandmother. I have to go and support her, she has supported us most of our lives. We can get together the next day. Is that going to be a problem?" She wants him to understand the importance of the day, so she tries to soften him up by speaking in a low and comforting voice.

However, his possessive and selfish ways prevent him from doing so. "Hell yeah that's gonna be a problem! You know that both of my parents are only out the house on Tuesday's. It's bad enough that we can't screw everyday. Therefore, we have to do what we can on Tuesday mornings because I can't miss my afternoon football practice's for any evening dates with you."

Stacy took a double look at Teddy and continued with her explanation in a sassy, but sympathetic tone. "Well, I don't know what to tell you. But what I do know is that my grandmother will be expecting me to be there to support her. There's no way I can tell her that I can't go. Besides, she doesn't ask much, so I have to go. Can't you understand that this is a very important day for her?"

"Well if you're gonna be my girl, you better find a way to show up or else!" he said with a demanding tone.

"Teddy, you're crazy!" She said with an attitude. Then she rolled her eyes in the air and folded her arms, while standing with a

Momma, Please Forgive Me!

lean, waiting for his next response.

Suddenly Teddy saw red, becoming furious. "Bitch! Who are you calling crazy?" Once he responded, Stacy could see the red in his eyes which caused her to become frightened. However, his reaction became even more frightening when he suddenly slapped her in her face, causing her face to turn red. She begins to cry and holds her face in amazement.

She then looks at him like he was crazy. "What did you do that for?"

Teddy got right in her face. Then he looked at her with a similar look to the one that her dad used to give her mom when he got mad. This look scared her even more, bringing back flashbacks of the fight that happened on the night he was killed.

Then he continued; "Ain't no damn body gonna call me crazy and get away with it, especially if it's my woman. So bitch, you better watch what you say to me or I'll kick up in your ass again, you got it?"

Stacy calmed her attitude way down. "I'm sorry. I won't say that again."

"Now, take your crying ass to class and when I say what you're gonna do, just expect to do it without a word. You got that bitch?" he continued with fury.

"I got it!" Stacy said with great fear. She knew from what her mother had experienced that this conversation was not leading to anything good. So, she kept quiet while he continued.

"Now get out of my damn face with all that baby ass crying. I gotta go to class. I can't be seen hanging around a baby. All I do know is that you better get it together if you want to be with me." Then he walked away, leaving her standing there crying more.

After he walked away she pulled out her mirror from her purse and looked at her red face. Then she reached for a tissue to wipe away the tears. While doing this, she began to seriously think about Teddy's actions and where their relationship was headed. "Why am I letting a man put his hands on me like that? This is the same shit that put my mother in prison. Why am I letting it happen to me? I should know better. Ain't no man worth taking hits from." Then she soften, giving an excuse for his fury. "But he's so cute. Maybe he just hit me because he loves me." Then she walked to her class, still wiping away the tears and touching up her mascara.

CHAPTER THIRTY-THREE

The time has come for La Vonne's appeal hearing. It's 8:30 in the morning. The entire family, including Stacy, Gloria's church friends and Pastor George are waiting for the judge to enter the courtroom. Sonny Waters is also present, just in case he's needed as a witness.

It's now 9 AM. The bailiff announces the entrance of the judge; "Everyone please rise for Judge Marian Webster." Everyone is stunned that the judge is an African-American woman. Her presence makes everyone feel hopeful, bringing smiles to their faces. She speaks in a very firm and confident manner, causing everyone to know that she takes her job very seriously. She portrays herself as a woman who's in control and not a pushover. She does not want anyone to think that because she's a woman, she's softer and more sympathetic with her cases.

The judge sits down in her big, black leather chair and proceeds with the hearing. "Please be seated so we can begin. Would the lawyer for defendant, La Vonne Brown, please stand and address the court."

Jay stands up, straightens his suite and tie and acknowledges the judge's request; "Good morning Your Honor. My name is attorney Bethel Jay Mitchell. I'm representing

Momma, Please Forgive Me!

Ms. La Vonne Brown this morning."

The judge shakes her head to acknowledge his response and proceeds; "Mr. Mitchell, I'm ready to hear your opening argument, proceed."

Everyone in the courtroom focuses their undivided attention on Jay. He gives an envelope to the bailiff, who gives the envelope to the judge. The envelope contains the evidence he has collected for his case. As she looks through it, he clears his throat to speak clearly and proceeds; "Your Honor, I would like to present new evidence for my client's case. Our evidence will prove that Mr. Jonathan Brown was in fact capable of committing cold-blooded murder. Your Honor, in that envelope are pictures of human bones found at Jack Stern's recreation center and park, which is located close to where the Mr. Brown once lived. You will notice that the bones are not fully in tact, they became deteriorated as a result of being exposed to various weather conditions. Your Honor, we've been able to gather evidence against Mr. Brown, which proves that he committed a murder prior to his untimely death. The pictures of the bones were traced back to a gentleman named, Ryan Dennison, who was reported missing over eleven years ago."

While Jay spoke, everyone held on to his every word, not wanting to miss any part of his opening statement as he continued; " Your Honor, Mr. Sonny Waters, who's seated in the rear of the courtroom has testified on tape that he was with Mr. Brown on the night he killed Ryan Dennison. Mr. Waters later went to police officials and attempted to tell his story of the killing, however, nothing was done. In fact, according to Mr. Waters, who is now a minister of God, stated that the officer he spoke with was quoted as saying; "Good, that's one less junky we have to worry about." Then he told Mr. Waters to forget about the murder and enjoy his new life. Mr. Waters' testimony is on the tape you have in your possession."

Then Jay proceeds to play a copy of the tape to the judge while everyone quietly listens. After playing the tape, everyone in the entire courtroom is stunned. The trial continues.

"Mr. Waters," the judge says while looking directly at Sonny Waters. "Can you come to the front of the courtroom and take an oath please? I need you to verify that those were in fact your words. Sonny rolled his wheelchair to the front of the courtroom and gave his oath. "Yes Your Honor. Those were my words."

"Mr. Waters, please state whether or not you were forced in any way to give that statement."

"No Your Honor, I was not forced in any way to say any of the words mentioned on that tape. They were all my own words."

"Mr. Waters, did Mr. Mitchell advise you that you were being taped while you gave your statement."

"Yes Your Honor I knew that the tape was running while I gave that statement."

"Thank you Mr. Waters. That's all. You may return to your seat. Counselor, you may proceed." the judge instructed.

To increase the dramatic and sympathetic mood in the courtroom, Jay moves away from the lawyers desk and paces the courtroom floor. "Thank you Your Honor. Your Honor, not only did my client have good reason to believe that she and her children were in danger, but Mr. Waters' confession proves that Mr. Brown did in fact kill a man while intoxicated with drugs and alcohol. Therefore, if the information was taken seriously and presued by the police when Mr. Dennison's family first reported his disappearance, Mr. Brown would have been arrested. His arrest would have resulted in his incarceration and Ms. Brown would not have had to fear for her own life and the life of her children. Therefore, it is assumed that it is also likely that Mrs. Brown

Momma, Please Forgive Me!

would not have been faced with the decision to end her husband's life in order to save the life of her family. So Your Honor, on behalf of Ms. Brown's family and myself, we would like you to release her from the custody of prison immediately. She has learned her lesson and needs to be at home, where she can raise her children and teach them to not make the same violent choices she made. Your Honor, at the time Ms. Brown believed that killing her husband was her only way out of an abusive situation. However, since that dreadful night, she has learned that her decision was wrong. She now wants an opportunity to prove that to her children and to the world. Your Honor, we thank you for hearing our case."

Then Jay slowly walked back to his seat and hoped for the best. Gloria had tears running down her face. La Vonne was trying to be strong and hold her tears.

"Thank you Counselor." The judge said after Jay finished his opening argument. Then she looked over her notes. The entire room was so quiet that you could have heard a pin drop. Then the judge looked at Jay, then at La Vonne and continued; "Mr. Mitchell, I have listened to your testimony. Now I'll review the entire case one last time and give you my ruling. Court will reconvene in one hour. Court is now adjourned." Then she hit her gavel on the stand and walked back to her chambers. Everyone in the courtroom was quiet, with somber looks on their faces. They were unsure if this was in fact going to be La Vonne's lucky day. La Vonne prayed it would be.

While the judge reviewed the case, La Vonne had to be escorted by a guard to a secured waiting room close by the courtroom. She was not allowed to wait with her family. She had a look of discouragement on her face as the guard took her away. While everyone watched La Vonne leave, the loud clinging sounds of her hand and leg chains made everyone feel uncomfortable. The tension level had reached great heights, keeping everyone on edge. "Grandma, why can't Momma stay in here with us until the judge comes back?' Stacy said with tears in her eyes.

Gloria hugged her granddaughter and tried to explain. "Baby, your mother is still considered a prisoner until the judge grants her release."

"But that's not fair." Jr. said, obviously upset.

"I know it isn't. But there's nothing we can do about it, but pray." Gloria said somberly while trying to also keep the faith herself. "So, I want you guys to try to be strong for your mother and just pray that the judge grants her a release. I'm sure that the judge just has to look over her notes and everything will be alright. I can feel it in my bones that everything will be alright. So just keep praying." Everyone continued holding each others hand and praying.

****

While everyone was in court, Teddy was at home waiting for Stacy to show up for their rendezvous. While waiting, Teddy is pacing the room, constantly looking out of his living room window, waiting for her to show up. He's upset that she has not arrived. His patience begins to wear short, causing him to become angry. "Where's that damn girl? I told her to bring her black ass over here. I bet she went to that damn center to see her damn grandma get some stupid award. Hell, I told her that I was her man and she needs to make sure my needs are taken care of first. Hell, her Grandma will bring her damn award home and then she can congratulate her old ass. Right now, I got needs that need to be taken care of, fuck her Grandma's feelings. But no, she did what she wanted to do. I'll fix her. Because ain't no bitch gonna stand me up! Hell, I'm Teddy Jones! Ladies wait for me, not the other ay around." Then he got his school stuff and stormed off, alone

Momma, Please Forgive Me!

and mad.

****

One hour later, court has reconvened. Everyone is now sitting in the courtroom, waiting for the judge to return. Then the bailiff stands to his feet and speaks; "All rise for Judge Marian Webster." he says firmly in his baritone voice.

The judge takes her seat and proceeds; "Be seated now." Then she looks at La Vonne and speaks; "I've reviewed the case and carefully listened to your recorded argument that was in your file from your first appeal. I'm now ready to give my verdict. Would the defendant, Ms. La Vonne Brown and counsel please stand to hear my verdict."

Jay stands. La Vonne looks around the entire room with expressions of fear on her face and slowly stands. Before she continues, the judge speaks with her firmly; "First of all Ms. Brown, taking the life of another human being was and is wrong. understand that you were abused. I also understand that you felt you had to do what you had to do in order to protect yourself and your children, as I am also a mother. However, murdering someone does not solve any problems, it only creates other problems. Ms. Brown I truly hope that you have learned your lesson on this matter."

La Vonne nervously speaks up as her hand begins to shake; "I definitely have learned Your Honor. I really have. And I'm truly sorry for what I did. I would never do anything like that again, ever!"

The judge looked at La Vonne with an unappealing look and responded; "Ms. Brown, I find this new evidence very interesting. Unfortunately, there are people in every profession who do not take their jobs seriously. Many of those people do not realize that the impact of what they say or do often results in pain and suffering for those who are either innocent, or those who have made bad choices. The officer involved in taking Mr. Waters complaint will have to answer for his actions later. Although, knowing that Mr. Brown was definitely capable of murder is sad. It's very sad to know that people actually allow drugs and alcohol to control their entire lives. However, that's a part of reality that we must try to change."

While the judge continued, La Vonne was unsure as to where her verdict was leading. The added pressure caused her hands to shake even more as sweat soaked her body, now becoming visible throughout her bright orange prison attire. La Vonne attempted to keep her composure while constantly praying for the best as the judge continued.

"Nevertheless, both of these realizations shed an entirely new light on this case. Had the chain of commands been handled differently, the outcome of the situation would been different. I must say that I sympathize with the Brown children for losing both of their parents. They lost one to the destruction of drugs and alcohol, and the other through imprisonment as a result of not receiving the needed help and guidance from law enforcement agencies. Therefore, I now grant the immediate release of Ms. La Vonne Brown out of Hallsworth County, Louisiana prison and into the hands of her family. You are now free to go home and raise your children properly. Teach them that violence is never the answer to a situation. Also, teach them to respect and abide by the law when things do go wrong."

The judge hit her gavel on the table and announced; "Court is dismissed." Then she walked out of the courtroom with a smile on her face while enjoying the cheers and cries from everyone in the room.

After hearing the words "free," La Vonne and her entire

family jumped into the air, loudly cheering for her freedom. La Vonne was finally able to cry, breaking down and crying like a baby. Her cries were felt deep down in her soul. A hugh weight had lifted off her heart. This was a day she had longed for, for over ten years. This was the day that God had smiled on her, allowing her to start her life over again. She was now feeling no pain, only gain. Then she grabbed and hugged Jay as tight as she could, kissing him on the cheek and spinning him in a circle.

"Oh Jay, Thank you! Thank you! Thank you! I would not have been able to do any of this without your help, so thank you a million times!" Then she kissed and hugged him again.

Jay was smiling so hard that you could see all of his pearly white teeth. He became so excited that he could hardly contain his professional manner. His cocky and comical behavior, which was often hidden, emerged; "Well what can I say? I'm just kidding, you're welcomed. I'm glad things turned out the way they did. But most of the credit goes to your cell-mate Sherri. Without her, you'd still be calling this place home. So make sure you thank her for all of us."

"Oh don't worry, I'll be sure to thank her when I go back to collect my belongings. But thank you for sticking by me and helping us when we didn't have the money to pay you. God is certainly good!"

"Yes he is!" Gloria jumped into the conversation while holding onto La Vonne as tight as she could; "God is definitely a good God! Jay, I want to also thank you for believing in my daughter. I thank God and Pastor George everyday for bringing you into our lives. You have really made a difference in all of our lives. A difference that we'll never forget. So I thank you from the bottom of my heart as well. And tonight I want you to come by the house so we can properly welcome La Vonne home."

"Alright, party over here!" Stacy added. Then Jr. spoke for both of them; "Jay, we also want to thank you for bringing our mother back home to us. We've missed her so much! We never thought this day would actually come." Then they hugged their mom as tight as they could while they all continued to cry.

"I thank all of you for the wonderful compliments. It's people like yourself that make my job worthwhile. And Amen, God is definitely a good God! So, I don't want any of you to worry about the money. I'm just glad I was able to help. God has already blessed me by helping you. Now, he'll bless me even more! So La Vonne, go with the guard and get your belongings. Then later, I'll meet all of you at your moms house to celebrate, and the champagne's on me. And next week, after you've had time to get used to being at home, I still want to take you out to dinner, if that's alright."

La Vonne blushed; "Of course it's alright!" she said with excitement. "So, we've got two dates! Tonight, for the welcome home celebration and dinner next week. But do me one big favor." "Anything, just name it."

"Can you change the champaign bubbly to sparkling apple cider? Alcohol is what attributed to me being here in the first place and I want to stay far away from anything or anyone who could ever bring me back. Coming back here is something I have no intentions in ever doing again!" Then everyone laughed through their tears.

"No problem, sparkling apple cider is what it'll be." Jay said while gathering his belongings so he could go back to his office and rap up the case.

"Ok, then I'll see you later tonight." La Vonne was still blushing. She couldn't believe that Jay still wanted to take her to dinner. She hoped for so long that a romantic relationship would spark up for them, when instead, only business existed. However,

Momma, Please Forgive Me!

with his invitation, she was beginning to feel hopeful; "This is the day that the Lord has truly made. Be glad in it." she thought as she looked into his eyes.

"I'll be there. So you guys take care and I'll see you tonight, bye." Jay said as he walked toward the exit.

"We'll be waiting." La Vonne yelled out as he was leaving. Suddenly she stopped in her tracks as she remembered the importance of the days date. As Jay approached the door, she called for him to come back, meeting him halfway. "Jay, Jay. Come back!" Jay stopped and walked back. "I need for you to do me one more very important favor please." He was surprised by her request as she quietly continued in private; "Ten years ago today; June 04, 1990, they buried my unborn twins. But they never told me where they were buried. Can you please find out where they are buried so I can pay my last respects to them please?" Then a tear fell from her eye.

Jay was taken by surprise by the request. "Sure, I'll do that for you. I remember seeing that information in your files when I first took on your case, but I didn't pay much attention to it, knowing that it wasn't the evidence we needed to help your case. I'll tell you what, by the time I get to the party, I'll have the information you need, how's that?"

Then she smiled; "That'll be just fine." Then Jay walked out the courtroom and La Vonne walked over to her family, the church ladies, who had helped support her mother throughout the ten years, becoming her best friends, and Pastor George. She gave her mother and children a big hug. Then she hugged Pastor George and the church ladies and thanked them for their continued support. Then the guard escorted her out of the courtroom to gather her belongings. "I'll see you guys at the check out area shortly."
La Vonne said while leaving the courtroom, still with tears streaming down her face. Her mother and children were also

crying while witnessing her departure. However, this time they accepted and welcomed her departure, because they knew that it would be her last departure from their lives.

CHAPTER THIRTY-FOUR

It's mid-afternoon. La Vonne has now entered the prison area where all the inmates are located. She knows that she is only there to collect her belongings which makes her feel on top of the world. As she walks in, yells as loud as she can; "I'm free everybody! I'm finally free! Today I'm going home!"

After hearing the good news, everyone in the area cheers her on; "Yeah! Yeah! You go girl. I wish I was going with you! Don't forget about us La Vonne." Everyone had something nice and different to say, making her feel proud.

"I won't! I won't forget any of you. I wish you all well! But I've gotta get the hell on out of here now before they change their mines!" she yelled back at them while laughing. After reaching her cell-room, she walked inside and smiled, knowing that this was her last day of living a life of pain. Trina the guard looked on, while La Vonne packed her belongings. While packing, La Vonne remembered her long stay in prison. In some sense she felt sad. This was the place she refused to call home, even though it had indeed been her home over ten years. Through those years, there were bad times, along with good times. She met friends, who became her family. She also feared others who she learned to avoid. After she gathered the few personal belongings she cared to take, leaving clothing with serial numbers behind, changing into some clothes her mother had brought just in case. La Vonne made one special stop to Sherri's cell. Sherri was very happy to hear the news.

Momma, Please Forgive Me!

La Vonne had big crocodile tears in her eyes as she spoke; "Sherri, I don't know how to thank you. The information you gave me is what set me free. For that, I will always be indebted to you. Thank you girl! I wish you all the best. Hopefully you'll get out of here soon. And when you do, please look me up. Until then, I'll be praying for you. I hope your stay is shortened, because you don't belong in a place like this either."

Sherri was also crying; "Girl, don't think about it. I'm just glad I was able to help you. I wish I had given you the information sooner. I'm glad you're able to get out of here and begin a whole new life with your kids, because they need their mother. Now, go on home to your babies and give them a big hug and kiss for me. Tell them I said hi and to take care of you for me. And when I get out, I'll make sure I look you up. Now go on girl, I can't let these folks see me cry like this. I have to continue living here. And you know by living here, you have to be strong. So go on and enjoy your life. You're a good person, you deserve every bit of happiness you can get!"

"I will and don't forget to look me up when you get out. I'll be waiting to hear from you. But I'll write until you get out. Maybe my letters will offer you a little encouragement until you're free. Since Sonny has forgiven you, maybe I can convince him to talk to a lawyer about reducing your sentence. Maybe Jay can help. Anyway, no matter what happens hang in there and stay strong. I'll always remember what you did for me and always thank you for doing it. So take care." La Vonne said as she hugged Sherri through the prison cell, with both of them crying like babies. Then La Vonne made her way toward the prison doors that would lead to her freedom.

After walking through several locked doors, she was about to taste freedom. "Well La Vonne, this is it." Trina the prison guard said while unlocking the hand and leg cuffs. "This is the last locked door you'll ever hear from this place. And I don't want to ever see you back here again. This is the beginning of a brand new world for you. So, go out and do something that will help someone else. Help those who may be on their way of coming here see the light, so that they don't ever make their way inside of a place like this. Help someone who may not be able to help themselves, like someone should have helped you when you were in need. Be the one to make a difference by doing something positive and keeping yourself real."

La Vonne was still crying, then she hugged Trina as tight as she could. She knew that she was lucky to have someone like her on her side to look out for her when she could. She also realized that her dream of freedom was finally coming. "Trina, thank you so much! Without your support and encouragement throughout the years, I would have been a total basket case. So, thank you so very much and I wish you well. Be careful and don't let anyone get the best of you."

Trina started laughing; "These girls ain't ever gonna get the best of me, I've been here far too long to let that happen! So, don't worry about me. You just take care of yourself and stay out of trouble!"

"You don't have to worry about me getting into any trouble, ever! I've learned my lesson. I don't ever want to see the inside of this place, or any prison again! So, until we meet again, I'll see ya when I see ya! But for real girl, I love you and thank you for all your kindness and support."

Trina was trying to not cry; "Girl, go on home before they change their minds and make you stay longer."

Then they both laughed; "Say no more, I'm out of here. Bye and take care."

"You take care too, bye!" Then the two hugged and La Vonne walked out of the prison, looked at the door that had shut tight, then at the high-wired walls, the opened blue sunlight sky, smiled, said a quick prayer and got into the car where her mother and children were waiting.

CHAPTER THIRTY-FIVE

It's four o'clock in the afternoon when Gloria pulls up in her driveway. Once the car has stopped, La Vonne begins to cry. She's very happy to finally be home. Jr. and Stacy start hugging her, welcoming her home.

"I can't believe it. I just can't believe that after ten long years I'm finally home." La Vonne said as she opened the car door and stepped outside, looking around the entire neighborhood. While admiring the view, tears of joy streamed steadily down her face. She soon made her way into the house with escorting hugs of support and security from her mom. Jr. gathered his mother's belongings and followed while Stacy stayed behind.

Stacy noticed that Teddy was waiting across the street, so she went to meet him. As she walked across the street, her gleaming smile spoke a thousand words of happiness for her mother's freedom, as well as the happiness she felt knowing that Teddy had finally stopped by to meet her family. While waiting in the courtroom, she had allowed herself a worthy explanation that would validate her mother's long disappearance. She was very happy to see Teddy, however, the look in his eyes told another story, causing her to become nervous. His expressions caused her approach him slowly, because she was unsure as to what was on his mind.

"Hi, I'm glad you stopped by to finally meet my family. Guess what, the most exciting and amazing thing just happened, my mother came home." she rambled, while gleaming with excitement as Teddy stood in silence. "She left when we were kids and no one knew where she was. My grandmother found her and surprised us by telling us that she was getting an award, when she was really taking us to pick up my mother."

"Bitch, fuck your momma!" Teddy roared with great fury. "Didn't I tell you to meet me at my house this morning?"

Suddenly Stacy froze with fear, causing her to stutter. "I, I, I hadddd to go, my grandmother made me."

"I don't give a fuck about what your grandma told you to do. I'm your man and when I tell you to do something, that's what you're suppose to do first. Standing me up is something that'll never happen again. You got it?" he said while pointing his finger directly in her face.

"Yeah." Stacy jumped back with elevated fear. As she watched the fury escalate in his eyes. His anger was another reminder of why her mother went to prison.

"So, come on. My parents haven't come home yet. You can see your momma later, after we're done taking care of our business." Then he pulled her wrist, to follow him. He was holding it so tight that it started turning red with pain.

"I can't go right now. My mother just came home." Stacy said while trying to unleash her wrist from his grasp. However, he continued to drag her toward his house, ignoring her comments. "I have to stay here with her. I'll come by tomorrow." However, the more she pulled, the more he pulled her toward him.

Suddenly he stopped and looked into her eyes with a violent glare. His grip on her wrist was so tight that she could now see bruises forming beneath the flaming red color of pain. "Look here bitch, either you come with me now, or it's over!" Then he dropped her wrist from the clutches of his hand.

After becoming free and realizing why her mother was in prison for so long, Stacy gained her composure and stood up to his fury. "You know Teddy, knowing everything my mother has been

Momma, Please Forgive Me!

through over the last fourteen years because of the abuse from a man is not worth the price she had to pay, resulting in her staying away from us. I see right now that you're an abuser. Anyone who'll call a woman out of her name, and disrespect her like you've disrespected me is not worth having, even if you are the most popular boy on campus. You're not worth my time, I deserve better! So, as far as I'm concerned, there is no US! I'll never let a man treat me like my father treated my mother, never! Besides, the way I see it, you seem to enjoy disrespecting women. I guess because of your strength and intimidation, you feel like a big man. Well you're not! And don't ever put your hands on me again!
"And another damn thing, if you're going to disrespect the people I love, than you're not worth my time anyway! So, consider our so-called relationship over! Like I said before, I deserve better than you'll ever be able to give me. And my family means more to me than you'll ever mean to me. So, when you learn how to respect a lady, maybe you'll find one. But you won't find her here!"

Stacy then turned around and walked away, leaving him standing alone and embarrassed. Due to the pride of his overinflated ego, that was the last straw. Tell him off and breaking up with him were things he was not going to let any woman get away with doing. After she walked away he became so furious that he ran to catch her, snatching her wrist again, pulling her back toward him. Then he slapped her in her face, knocking her down to the ground and making her lip bleed. "Bitch, I told you about dissing me. Ain't no damn woman gonna talk to me like that and walk away."

While Stacy laid on the ground crying and wiping the blood from her lip, her eyes grew with added fear as she watched his fury continue to explode. "You crazy bitch, shut up! Quit all that damn crying! I'm out of here." Teddy left her laying on the ground and started walking away.

Suddenly, Jr. ran from across the street, catching up to Teddy and knocked him down to the ground. While Teddy is laying on the ground, recovering from what hit him, Jr. begins to hit Teddy so hard that he bleeds. As Jr. fights with Teddy, flashes of his mother and father fighting appear in his head. These flashes are the one's that have surfaced in his dreams many times before. The more the flashes appeared, the more Jr. hits Teddy. Stacy gets up and tries to stop the fight, but she can't, as Jr. is out for revenge. His revenge is aimed toward Teddy, but in reality, he was paying his father back for all the times he beat their mother. So Stacy screams for help.

After hearing the loud screams from Stacy, La Vonne runs from across the street to stop the fight. She begins yelling and pulling Jr. off of Teddy. The adrenalin and anger stored up in La Vonne's body over the last fourteen years has given her petite five foot high, 120 pound body the strength needed to pull her six foot tall, 190 pound son apart from Teddy's five foot, seven inch high, 165 pound body. "Stop all this fighting, stop it now! I just got out of prison and have seen enough violence to last me several lifetimes!"

Jr. is fuming and breathing hard with his fist still balled tight. "He slapped Stacy in the face." Jr. roared. Teddy looked up, almost unaware to where he was. He was shocked to hear the word prison come out of La Vonne's mouth. Then La Vonne looks directly into Teddy's eyes as he slowly gets up off the ground, wiping the dirt from his clothes and the blood from his face.

"And whoever you are, don't ever put your damn hands on my daughter again! Boy don't you know that abuse is what put me in prison ten years ago? I know what hatred and abuse did to me and I'm not going to let my daughter go down the same road I went through with her father. Boy don't you know that violence is not the solution to anything? Besides, hitting a lady is the last thing you should be thinking about doing in the first place. Your parents should have taught you how to respect a lady. But since they

Momma, Please Forgive Me!

didn't, you ain't gonna disrespect my daughter! So, if you hit her again I'll report you to the authorities, and believe me, this time they'll come running! And when they come, you'll get a taste of how it feels to be hit by someone much bigger and stronger than you are. And if you call yourself a man you ain't! Because a real man would never hit a woman, no matter how angry he got. So, get away from my daughter and don't ever let me see you around her again, because I'm back and I'll never let her make the same mistakes I made with her father. So kids, lets not waste our time with the likes of him. Lets go back in the house and celebrate. I'm back and I'm never leaving any of you again!"

"I'm really sorry Stacy," Teddy says with humiliation. "I'm also sorry to you Ms. Brown. I guess I was just trippin', even though that's not an excuse. I promise that that'll never happen again. I guess I wasn't thinking. Jr., you got a real woman for a sister, sorry man." Then Teddy reached his hand out to Jr. to shake and Jr. accepted his apology with hesitation. They shook hands and Teddy slowly walked to his house, still bleeding and wiping the dripping blood on his clothes.

La Vonne put her arms around Stacy and Jr. and together they walked back to the house. The excitement of the fight brought out the neighbors who welcomed La Vonne's return. Everyone followed La Vonne back to Gloria's house where they all celebrated her return from prison for the rest of the night, leaving everything that happened in the past, in the past.

****

After the celebration settled down, Jay delivered the requested information La Vonne wanted on her twins. He offered to take her to the burial site so that she could pay her last respects. The summer night was unusually dark and cold.

While driving the twenty mile distance it took to get to the burial site, La Vonne remained very quiet. The drive felt like her entire lifetime was passing by, causing her body to feel the emptiness of her baby's precious little soul's. As she sat in deep thought, she visualized the harsh pain she endured, as the tiny bodies of her unborn twins hemorrhaged out of her body on that fateful night. She had not only lost her husband, whom she once loved and adored, but she had also lost the two tiny bodies that she had felt for six long months growing in her body. The very thought made her cry in silence.

While trying to understand and sympathize with the pain La Vonne was feeling, Jay remained quiet, respecting her mood, leaving her to her sentimental thoughts.

Upon arriving at the designated burial site, La Vonne took a deep breath as Jay pointed out the exact spot with his flashlight. "Come on, let me walk with you," he offered as he put his coat over her arms to keep her warm. "It's dark and cold out here. I don't want you to do this alone."

"No thank you." La Vonne responded in a somber tone. "I need to do this on my own. Don't worry about me, I'll be alright. Besides, no one's here right now, and you can see me from where you're parked. Everything will be Ok. Stay in the car and keep warm. I'll be right back." La Vonne opened the car door and stepped out.

"Wait, take the flashlight so you can see where you're going. That field is very dark." Jay told her as he gave her the flashlight.

"Thank you." she said and smiled. "I'll be back." Then she made her way up the dark hill, in search of the resting place of her twins.

Once she arrived at the grave-site, La Vonne noticed that the area was only marked with a small metal imprint that replaced the tombstone of their resting place, along with several unknown

Momma, Please Forgive Me!

babies. The marker only held a long identification number that included several letters. It also read... June 24, 1990, twenty days after their actual birth.

"My babies! My babies!" she cried out loud as she kneeled on the cold wet grass. "My babies are gone!" Then her voice lowered as she begin to have a serious conversation with God. "Why did he have to kill my babies? Lord, only you know why this had to happen. Maybe one day you'll help me understand, because right now understanding is a long way away. For now, I give my thanks to you that my babies are safe and in your arms. If they would have lived, they may not have been healthy, due to the many beatings I endured while carrying them in my womb. Lord, thank you for allowing the judge to see the light by granting my freedom. Please bless me and my family as we continue through life, trying to pick up the lost pieces left behind. Babies, mommy loves you and will always keep you close to my heart. In Jesus' name, Amen!"

Suddenly, after La Vonne raised her head from her prayer, a noise was heard, coming from the nearby tree which perched directly behind the grave-site. La Vonne panicked and quickly shined her flashlight toward the direction in which it was heard. After her eyes became focused to the dimly lit shadow, to her surprise appeared to be Jonathan standing in the darkness smiling, while holding a single red rose. She was in total shock and could not scream out. Her voice was deadened, allowing Jonathan to quietly and calmly speak; "Welcome home La Vonne, I've been waiting for you." The sound of his voice paralyzed her, causing her drop the flashlight and faint on the cold wet grass, where she laid alone, next to her unborn babies final resting place.

The End!

AUTHOR'S NOTE

Now, that you have read this book, if you know anyone, including yourself, who is, or has experienced domestic, drug or alcohol abuse, know that their are people willing to help. Don't let the silent killer allow you to make the wrong choice. Be socially responsible to others and to yourself by doing the right thing and seek help. Don't keep turning the other way, hoping and praying that things will get better. Take the time to let down your guard and talk to someone you trust, someone who cares. Get help before it's too late, or before the unthinkable happens.

According to the National Coalition Against Domestic Violence, Public Health Reports, and Health Words for women & The National Domestic Violence Hotline. Domestic Violence is considered as the leading cause of injuries to women.

According to findings by the Surgeon General, domestic violence is the leading cause of injury to women between ages 15 to 24, more common than automobile accidents, muggings, and cancer deaths combined. Every 15 seconds, a woman is battered in the United States by her husband, boyfriend, or live-in partner.

One-fifth to one-third of all women are physically abused during their lifetime. Ten percent of the time the injury is serious enough to require hospitalization or emergency room treatment. The combination of physical and psychological symptoms that occur in women who suffer chronic abuse is known medically as the battered woman syndrome.

Physicians can't always recognize the physical symptoms of abuse without help from the victims themselves. Many abused women have difficulty in admitting it because of fear, guilt, or shame that they may feel, or because of a deep-seated denial that they are abused.

Every year, domestic violence results in almost 100,000 days of hospitalizations, almost 30,000 emergency department visits, and almost 40,000 visits to a physician.

With an estimated rate of a woman being battered every 15 seconds, twenty-two to 35 percent of these women who do visit emergency departments in the United States have ongoing symptoms of abuse. An estimated 90 percent of all domestic violence incidents go unreported.

Studies reveal that 40 to 80 percent of the time alcohol is a factor in incidents of domestic violence. However, researchers agree that alcohol is not the cause of domestic violence. However, drinking lowers one's control or inhibitions and may be the excuse for letting down these restraints against violence.

A new study released by the Journal of the American Medical Association reports that 1 in 5 teenage girls are physically or sexually abused by a dating partner. They suggest that young teens who are abused by a dating partner are at increased risk of suicide, drug abuse and other harmful behavior. The statistic is that 1 in 3 teenagers are abused by a partner because of emotional, fiscal and mental and social abuse.

According to WEAVE - There are ways in which someone can predict whether they are about to become involved with someone who has the potential of being physically abusive. If a person has several of the following behaviors, there is a strong potential for physical violence in the relationship. Signs to look for in a battering personalities include: Jealousy, Controlling Behavior, Quick Movement, Unrealistic Expections, Isolation, and Blames Other for His Problems.

The CDC justifies these signs as using; Power and Controlling traits, such as; Using Intimidation, Coercion and Threats, Economic Abuse, Male Privilege, Children, Minimizing Denying and Blaming, Isolation and Emotional Abuse. So, don't be a victim, help is out there for you, your family or friends. Listed are a few telephone numbers and web sites that can begin the healing. So, take the time by taking one of the biggest steps of your life and get help!

HELP - HOTLINE NUMBERS

National Domestic Violence Hotline 1-800-799-SAFE (7233) This hotline is staffed 24 hours a day by trained counselors who can provide crisis assistance and information about shelters, legal advocacy, health care centers, and counseling.

W.E.A.V.E. Women Escaping A Violent Environment: Call collect: (916) 920-2952 This organization also has a 24 hour hotline, assisted by trained counselors who can assist with you questions and/or concerns about domestic violence.

Institute on Domestic Violence in the African American Community (877) 643-8222 This Institute's mission is to provide, prevent/reduce family violence in the African American community by offering public speaking and awareness workshops.

Jenesse Center, Inc. (800) 479-7328 www.jenessecenter.org This Center provides victims, teens and adults, with a comprehensive, centralized base of support.

Watershed Drug & Alcohol Treatment Center (800) 711-6375 This hotline is staffed 24 hours a day by trained counselors who can provide crisis assistance and information regarding drug and alcohol concerns.

Web Site Listings

U.S. Department of Justice: www.usdoj.gov/ domesticviolence.htm This web site has valuable information on domestic violence.

Centers For Disease Control and Prevention (CDC) www.cdc.gov/ncipc.dvp.fivpt/spotlite.power.htm This web site has valuable information on domestic violence.

COVER PAGE ARTIST

Brian Olsen
Professional Freelance Artist

Brian Olsen has had a pencil and paper in his hands since he was born! He loves to draw, has always loved art and will always be dedicated to his craft. His career plans include having a prosperous career in the field of arts. He is currently a college art student and plans to farther and achieve an educational degree in this field.

"I would like to thank my sister Lori for setting up this great opportunity. I would like to thank my mom (Karen) and dad (Ron) for their love and unconditional support. I would like to thank my brother Eric for teaching me 80% of my drawing skills, and my loving girlfriend Whitney. I would also like to thank Toi for this incredible opportunity and for all of her patience. Thank you!"

Brian Olsen can be contacted by:
TM Publications
PO Box 443
Colton, CA 92324
B O ILLuStRaToR@aol.com

Freeway
Lincoln-Mercury VW, Inc.
Charles E. McVay
Owner/Operator
1600 Camino Real
San Bernardino, CA 92408
Bus: (909) 889-3514
Fax: (909) 885-6494
Toll Free: (800) 237-8115
Web: freewaylm-vw.com

****

Woman to Woman
Obstetrics and Gynecology Medical Group, Inc.

Betty Steward Daniels, M.D.
Irene Donley-Kimble, M.D.
Diplomate of American Board
of Obstetrics and Gynecology

249 E. Highland Ave. San Bernardino, CA 92404
(909) 881-1683
17171 Foothill Blvd. Ste. C Fontana, CA 92335
(909) 428-3457
1800 Western Ave. Ste. 204 San Bernardino, CA 92411
(909) 473-1401
8:00 am to 6:00 pm - By Appointment Only

D' Graphics Publications, Inc.

At D' Graphics Publications, Inc. (DGP), we have one singular objective - To be obedient to God's word. We have dedicated our lives and business to spreading the gospel.

Husband and Wife team, Andre' and Debra Holley, seek the Lord daily. They are ever alert to the spiritual warfare that continues to try to decieve and distract Christians from praising The Father and reaping the benefits of a godly life.

The Bookpoem Christian Poetry Bookmark collection and calendars, created by the inspirational words of Andre' and specially designed by Debra, are one way they share God's gifts He gave them. The corresponding scripture on the back of the bookmarks gives them confirmation of the origin of these thoughts.

"It is our prayer that the soothing nature of this collection will be as uplifting for you as it has been for us, our family, and friends. As you enjoy these gifts, we also pray that you share them with others. May God bless you with His perfect peace." Andre' and Debra Holley

D' Graphics also creates: Brochures, Logo Design, Flyers, Personalized Calendars, Personalized Bookmarks, Wedding Invitiations and more!

They can accomadate large or small orders.
For more information contact:

D' Graphics Publications, Inc.
(909) 469-9868 or fax (909) 865-1802
PO Box 4957
Diamond Bar, CA 91765
Email: dgraphics1@juno.com

Quick Order Form
Momma, Please Forgive Me!

Mail orders to: TM Publications, Orders Department
PO Box 443, Colton, CA 92324

Please Print:

Name:_____

Addresss:_____

City:_____State_____Zip_____

Telephone:(   )_____

Email
Adress:_____

Cost of book:

$13.95 ea. US / plus $3.00 for shipping within the US
Total: $16.95 US dollars
$20.50 ea. Canada / plus $5.00 shipping within Canada
Total:$25.50 US dollars

Sales Tax: Add 7.75% for products shipped to California.
Shipping Charges: 1st book $3.00, $2.00 for each additional book.
Next day mail add $15.00 for postage within US. 2nd day mail add $5.00 for postage within the US.

Make Checks or MO's payable to
TM Publications
Visit our Website at www.toimoore.com

Name:_____

Address:_____

City/State/Zip:_____

Postage

TM Publications
ATTN: Orders Dept.
PO Box 443
Colton, CA 92324

Quick Order Form
Momma, Please Forgive Me!

Mail orders to: TM Publications, Orders Department
PO Box 443, Colton, CA 92324

Please Print:

Name:_____

Addresss:_____

City:_____State_____Zip_____

Telephone:(   )_____

Email
Adress:_____

Cost of book:

$13.95 ea. US / plus $3.00 for shipping within the US
Total: $16.95 US dollars
$20.50 ea. Canada / plus $5.00 shipping within Canada
Total:$25.50 US dollars

Sales Tax: Add 7.75% for products shipped to California.
Shipping Charges: 1st book $3.00, $2.00 for each additional book.
Next day mail add $15.00 for postage within US. 2nd day mail add $5.00 for postage within the US.

Make Checks or MO's payable to
TM Publications
Visit our Website at www.toimoore.com

Name:_____

Address:_____

Postage

City/State/Zip:_____

TM Publications
**ATTN: Orders Dept.
PO Box 443
Colton, CA 92324**

Always Remember!

Always remember that the
sky is our ONLY limit!!
And God can give us
the world if we work hard
toward achieving
our goal!

Keep working hard,
Never give up and
Always follow and believe
your heart and
your dreams!
Your goals will eventually
come to the light!

The rest will be easy!

Toi

You don't have to be a victim!